T0362918

**PUBLISHED BY BOOM BOOKS**

boombooks.biz

## ABOUT THIS SERIES

....But after that, I realised that I knew very little about these parents of mine. They had been born about the start of the Twentieth Century, and they died in 1970 and 1980. For their last 20 years, I was old enough to speak with a bit of sense.

I could have talked to them a lot about their lives. I could have found out about the times they lived in. But I did not. I know almost nothing about them really. Their courtship? Working in the pits? The Lock-out in the Depression? Losing their second child? Being dusted as a miner? The shootings at Rothbury? My uncles killed in the War? Love on the dole? There were hundreds, thousands of questions that I would now like to ask them. But, alas, I can't. It's too late.

Thus, prompted by my guilt, I resolved to write these books. They describe happenings that affected people, real people. The whole series is, to coin a modern phrase, designed to push your buttons, to make you remember and wonder at things forgotten.

The books might just let nostalgia see the light of day, so that oldies and youngies will talk about the past and re-discover a heritage otherwise forgotten. Hopefully, they will spark discussions between generations, and foster the asking and answering of questions that should not remain unanswered.

# BORN IN 1955?
## WHAT ELSE HAPPENED?

## RON WILLIAMS

### AUSTRALIAN SOCIAL HISTORY

### BOOK 17 IN A SERIES OF 35
### FROM 1939 to 1973

War Babies Years (1939 to 1945):   7 Titles
Baby Boom Years (1946 to 1960):   15 Titles
Post Boom Years (1961 to 1970):   13 Titles

### BOOM, BOOM BABY, BOOM

# BORN IN 1955?  WHAT ELSE HAPPENED?

Published by Boom Books.

Wickham, NSW, Australia

Web: www.boombooks.biz

Email: jen@boombooks.biz

Creator: Williams, Ron, 1934- author

Title: Born in 1955? : what else happened? / Ron Williams.

ISBN: 9780994601551(paperback)

Series: Born in series, book 17.

Australia--History--Miscellanea--20th century.

Cover images: Mitchell Library: National Library of Australia

7_43372LF, Frank and Nancy Sinatra at Mascot;

A12111, 1/1955/32/16, migrant arrivals;

A1200, L19342, girls and doll;

A1501, A246/3, bush picnic.

# CONTENTS

# IMPORTANT PEOPLE AND EVENTS

| | |
|---|---|
| Queen of England | Elizabeth II |
| Oz Prime Minister | Bob Menzies |
| Leader of Opposition | Doc Evatt |
| The Pope | Pope Pius XII |
| US President | Dwight Eisenhower |

## PM OF BRITAIN:

| | |
|---|---|
| Until April 25 | Winston Churchill |
| After April 25 | Anthony Eden |

## WINNERS OF THE ASHES:

| | |
|---|---|
| 1954-55 | England   3-1 |
| 1956 | England   2-1 |
| 1958-59 | Australia   4-0 |

## MELBOURNE CUP WINNERS:

| | |
|---|---|
| 1954 | Rising Fast |
| 1955 | Toparoa |
| 1956 | Evening Peal |

## 1955 ACADEMY AWARDS:

Best Actor: Ernest Borgnine (Marty)

Best Actress: Anna Mangani (The Rose Tatoo)

# EVENING RADIO SHOWS, 1955

The old popular radio serials like *Yes What*, *Dad and Dave* and *Martin's Corner* had all gone, although the ABC's *Blue Hills* hung in there for years to come.

The evening news was on at 7pm on most stations. Before then, there was a range of soporific music from Clive Amadio.

After the news, the ever popular Jack Davey Show dominated the air-waves, with his call of *Hi Ho Everybody, This is Jack Davey*. Later, a few US shows like *Ellery Queen Mysteries* and the *Frankie Lane* Show got a mention.

Religion had a small role. On Catholic 2SM, the Angelus took up five minutes at 6 o'clock, and almost every station had a meditation for 5 minutes before signing off for the night, at about 11 or 12.

A popular Thursday night show was the *Amateur Hour* where, each week, local talent got a chance to impress the audience. The winner for the week was decided by mail-in votes, so there was the occasional scandal when some group colluded to vote for a performer of their choice, regardless of merit. Good clean fun.

Late in the evening, the first of the shock jocks, Eric Baume, stirred the masses. More fun.

Note that there are no TV shows listed. This is because Australia did not get TV until just before the start of the 1956 Olympic Games.

## PREFACE TO THIS SERIES:  1939 TO 1973

This book is the 17th in a series of books that I aim to publish. It tells a story about a number of important or newsworthy events that happened in 1955. **The series** will cover each of the years from 1939 to 1970, for a total of thirty-two books, which should just about bring me to the end of my thoroughly undistinguished writing career.

I developed my interest in writing these books a few years ago at a time when my children entered their teens. My own teens started in 1947, and I started trying to remember what had happened to me then. I thought of the big events first, like Saturday afternoon at the pictures, cricket in the back yard, and the wonderful fun of going to Maitland on the train for school each day. Then I recalled some of the not-so-good things. I was an altar boy, and that meant three or four Masses a week. I might have thought I loved God at that stage, but I really hated His Masses. And the schoolboy bullies, like Greg Fennell, and the hapless Freddie Evers. Yet, to compensate for these, there was always the beautiful, black headed, blue-sailor-suited June Browne, who I was allowed to worship from a distance.

I also thought about my parents. Most of the major events that I lived through came to mind readily. But after that, I realised that I really knew very little about these parents of mine. They had been born about the start of the Twentieth Century, and they died in 1970 and 1980. For their last 20 years, I was old enough to speak with a bit of sense. I could have talked to them a lot about their lives. I could have found out about the times they lived in. But I did not. I know almost nothing about them really.

Their courtship? Working in the pits? The Lock-out in the Depression? Losing their second child? Being dusted as a miner? The shootings at Rothbury? My uncles killed in the War? There were hundreds, thousands of questions that I would now like to ask them. But, alas, I can't. It's too late.

Thus, prompted by my guilt, I resolved to write these books. They describe happenings that affected people, real people. In **1955,** there is some coverage of international affairs, but a lot more on social events within Australia. This book, and the whole series is, to coin a modern phrase, designed to push the reader's buttons, to make you remember and wonder at things forgotten. The books might just let nostalgia see the light of day, so that oldies and youngies will talk about the past and rediscover a heritage otherwise forgotten. Hopefully, they will spark discussions between generations, and foster the asking and the answering of questions that should not remain unanswered.

**The sources of my material.** I was born in 1934, so I can remember well a great deal of what went on around me from 1939 onwards. But of course, the bulk of this book's material came from research. This meant that I spent many hours in front of a computer reading electronic versions of newspapers, magazines, Hansard, Ministers' Press releases and the like. My task was to sift out, **day-by-day,** those stories and events that would be of interest to most readers. Then I supplemented these with materials from books, broadcasts, memoirs, biographies, government reports and statistics. And I talked to old-timers, one-on-one, and in organised groups, and to Baby Boomers about their recollections. People with stories to tell come out of the woodwork, and talk no end about the tragic and funny and commonplace events that have shaped their lives.

**The presentation of each book.** For each year covered, the end result is a collection of short Chapters on many of the topics that concerned ordinary people in that year. I think I have covered most of the major issues that people then were interested in. On the other hand, in some cases I have dwelt a little on minor frivolous matters, perhaps to the detriment of more sober considerations. Still, in the long run, this makes the book more readable, and hopefully it will convey adequately the spirit of the times.

Each of the books is mainly Sydney based, but I have been **deliberately national in outlook**, so that readers elsewhere will feel comfortable that I am talking about matters that affected them personally. After all, housing shortages and strikes and juvenile delinquency involved all Australians, and other issues, such as problems overseas, had no State component in them. **So, I expect I can make you wonder, remember, rage and giggle equally, no matter where you hail from.**

## CARRY-OVER STORIES FROM 1954

In my previous 1954 book, I followed **the biggest story of that year**. It involved **Herbert Evatt (Doc)** and his wild and woolly involvement in the Petrov Affair. I should tell you at this stage that Evatt was now the leader of the Australian Labor Party, which was in Opposition in Parliament.

In previous lives, he had been the youngest judge ever appointed to the High Court of Australia, and had also been the third President of the United Nations General Assembly. You can see that he was a most distinguished and intelligent lawyer.

Yet, he was erratic. For one thing, he was zealous about any cause he pursued, and inclined to let idealism interfere with more practical considerations. Last year, in 1954, he was hell-bent on doing what Opposition leaders aspire to, and that was to destroy the Government. He thought he had a good chance because the Government of Bob Menzies had opened a Royal Commission that was supposedly likely to expose extensive spying in Australia by the nasty and destructive Russian Communists.

Almost everyone in the nation was rather tickled at the thought that we had our very own spies, though there was much derision levelled at the idea we had any secrets that the Russians wanted. Evatt, though, saw this as a big opportunity to embarrass the Government, and jumped into the politics of the Royal Commission with much elan.

The Commission had a series of public hearings, and I reported on these in my 1954. Let me sum up, though, by saying that Evatt, interfering at every stage, made a complete mess of everything he did, and came out of the Petrov Affair with his reputation in tatters.

By the end of 1954, most of the public interest in this skulduggery had disappeared. There was a final report to come, and its recommendations for action, but nobody who had read the transcripts expected much from that. So it seemed that the Petrov Affair would pass into history, with no one found guilty of anything, and no scalps taken.

But, Dr Evatt was not a man to give up on an idea that had obsessed him for a year. So that much later in the year, he did one of the silliest things that had ever been done in Parliament. I will not spoil that story by telling you more details here, but will **come back to it live** as the year goes on.

## MENZIES

Menzies was the Leader of the Liberal Party, and held enough seats in Parliament to not worry about passing his Bills. He had all the self-control that Evatt lacked, he was always considered and eloquent in whatever he spoke about, he was never flustered, and was building quite a reputation as a Statesman, rare for Australian politicians.

His main **obvious** policy was to get rid of the Reds wherever they turned up. So, with every sign of a major strike, he pointed out the evils that Reds do, and nicely turned their strike into a platform for recruiting supporters. Behind that, he wanted Australia to grow by promoting trade, he wanted social services to be adequate and never generous, and he wanted to watch as much cricket as possible. He admired Queen Elizabeth II greatly, and was emphatic in his loyalty to Britain and the Empire. He looked like he was here to stay, as Prime Minister, for a long time.

## OTHER CONTINUING STORIES FROM 1954

Every morning, right round the nation, families sat down for their Rice Bubbles, and turned on the wireless. Every morning they found out that someone or other would not be performing his job that day, because he was on an impromptu strike. This raised the question of whether **regular, monotonous and persistent strikes** can be seen as impromptu. Whatever the answer, the strikes kept coming, day after day, and effected one service after another.

The reason **might** have been that the workers were so persecuted by their bosses that they had no alternative but to fight against their oppression by striking. There **might** have occasionally have been some truth in this assertion, but it would be closer to the mark to say that some Communist shop-steward or Union boss was able to bring work to a halt for a while.

Why would anyone do this so capriciously? Our Trade Unions were dominated by Communists. These latter were well organised, dedicated, and prepared to go out on a limb to further their cause. **What was their cause? Some of the Reds** simply admired the system existing in the Soviet Union where all workers produced the "fruits of Labor" that went to the commune and were divided among the workers. Of course, it was much more sophisticated than this, but that was the principle.

**Other Reds had much more dangerous ideas**. They **added in** the philosophy of Karl Marx who wrote that such a situation could be brought about only by first crippling the existing nation, and then imposing the revolutionary new system in its stead. So **these Reds were working to cripple the nation**, and hence the strikes.

I hope that such serious talk is not too much for you so early in the book. I promise you that when I come back to strikes, I will give you more time to breathe. In the meantime though, I ask you to keep in mind, as we proceed, that daily strikes were a constant menace and frustrated everyone every day.

## UNREST  STORIES FROM 1954

Two major themes were apparent. **The first** was the ongoing battle between the goodies and the baddies, also known as Communism and Capitalism. Or the other way round if you like. Whatever you decide, the Russians and the Americans were locked into what would become a 40-year battle of ideologies, where each of them said that **it was better in all respects than its opposite number**, and **if** a war broke out, it could belt the living daylights out of its opponent.  But, each of them **also** contended, **it** was benign and friendly and charitable to all and sundry, and any nation would be wise to align fully with it.

Australia was firmly in the American camp as far as foreign policy was concerned.  We were laconically committed to the capitalist philosophy, and in practice were happy enough to follow America's lead in international affairs. But the urgency and frenetic worry that marked such matters in the US was absent in Oz.

**The second theme** was seen in the efforts of dozens and dozens of small nations to be free of their colonial masters. During the War, the passion for independence among these nations had grown, and in this post-war era almost every one of them was at some stage or other in its fight to control its own destiny. Whether it was the dark nations of Africa, or the hundreds of former Dutch islands of Indonesia, or the great British Dominion of India, every one of them wanted to be freed from their former British, Dutch and French masters.

This meant that the news was full, day after day, of reports of incidents between the dominant white rich exploiters (or developers, if you like) and the poor oppressed native populations, of dozens of nations. In fact, most often, the colonial powers were coming to accept that it was time to move out, but inevitably the transfer of power was taking too long, so that violence on the ground was common.

In Australia, once again, we could watch with interest. Such unrest was a long way from our shores. We did have our own problems with Aborigines in Oz. And we had potential difficulties with the natives in New Guinea. But neither of these races was militant at the moment, and so again Australia remained a nice comfortable haven from which to observe the world.

**Comment.** I must admit that the last page was taken pretty much unchanged from the **Introduction** to my previous *1954* book. When I now came to summarise the unrest and dissension in the world, I concluded that nothing much had altered, and I could not think of ways of improving on my previous year.

It does, however, bring home to me the insularity of our Australian world at this time. I was able to write a 1954 summary of international events, and then use it almost holus bolus for the next year. **Does that mean that nothing has changed?** Does it mean that all the big wars and little battles and all the agitating and demonstrations and all the independence movements, had left the world unchanged?

**No it does not**. It just means that **we** were so far removed from it all that we were simply observers, and generally, we were disinterested observers. **Here**, we could simply sit back and watch with interest as the Chinese built up their forces. And **here** we could take with a yawn the news that the goodies and baddies were once again nearly coming to blows over the occupation of West Berlin. It all seemed too remote to worry about, and who would be mad enough to actually start fighting over such disputes? No, we unconsciously thought, it will not worry us, and even if we worried about it day and night, what good could **we** do?

## MY RULES IN WRITING

**NOTE.** In this book, I often re-produce Letters from the newspapers. Whenever I do this, I put the text in a different font, and indent it a little, and make the font somewhat smaller. **I do not edit the text at all**. That is, I do not correct spelling or grammar, and if the text gets at all garbled, I do not correct it. It's just as it was seen in the Papers.

**SECOND NOTE.** My material, when it comes from newspapers, is reported as it was seen at the time. If the benefit of hindsight over the years changes things, then I **might** record that in my **Comments**. The info reported thus reflects matters **as they were seen in 1955**.

**THIRD NOTE. Let me apologise in advance to anyone I might offend**. In a work such as this, it is certain some people will think I got some things wrong. I am certain I did, but please remember, all of this is **only my opinion**. And really, **my opinion does not matter one little bit in the scheme of things. I hope you will say "silly old bugger", shrug your shoulders, and read on.**

# JANUARY NEWS ITEMS

**What a way to start a year.** In the cricket versus England, in the Third Test, at the hallowed Boxing Day Test in Melbourne, **Australia collapsed on the last day,** with the last eight wickets falling for only 36 runs. **Oh the pain!!**

**The introduction of beer gardens** into hotels was raising questions. Everyone knew that children were not allowed into bars. **But was a beer garden a bar?** Many such gardens did not have a formal bar, and drinks were brought out to patrons by a roving waiter. **Would children be damaged** by playing at the feet of mothers drinking in a beer garden?

A New Zealand man spent the **last 21 days sitting on a clutch of four hen eggs.** Despite reproducing the correct conditions, he **was unable to hatch any chickens, and he sadly admitted that hens can do it better.**

**Overseas entertainers were flooding into Oz to perform to hordes of screaming teens.** The latest arrivals were **Dan Rowan and Dick Martin**, who were well known here from their silly and funny TV show. They performed at Sydney Stadium in the first half of a double bill, and were "noisily barracked by a section of the audience for being on the stage too long"....

**The second performer was Nat King Cole.** He was received with enthusiasm and was, **as expected in those days**, and **mobbed by teenage girls** on completion of his act. "Your audiences are sensational. When you get a nice audience like that, you don't mind giving encores."

**Six horses went to sea in the freighter *Port Alma* equipped with sea-boots, lifebelts, and a 200-yard carpet.** The horses were bound for the 1956 Olympic Games equestrian events in Stockholm, 12,000 miles away....

The sea-boots and carpets were to prevent them from **slipping on the decks on their daily walks. The life belts were in case the ship has to be abandoned.** They are bound initially for Gloucestershire in England, where they will spend 18 months in acclimatising and training for next year's Olympics

The effects of **the new liquor trading laws** in NSW are starting to become apparent. Ten Sydney hotels, near the wharves and markets, have applied for early opening licences starting at 6am....

The new laws provide for the granting of licences to **clubs with a membership of 100 or more.** Clubs everywhere were asking themselves whether they wanted to be licensed. These included sporting clubs such as bowling clubs, RSLs, and Workers clubs. **It was the beginning of a new era.** Other States were either following or leading NSW.

A week after Nat King Cole, **Frank Sinatra** flew into Sydney on his way to Melbourne. Although he was in the airport for less that an hour, **he was greeted by 10,000 fans**, "the largest crowd ever seen at Sydney airport." **The rapture continued when he got to Melbourne but there was no swooning.**

# JANUARY: AUSTRALIA ON HOLS

Every year since the war, Australia has taken its "Christmas" holidays seriously. For most of January, the work-force and its families stop working, and instead loll about, superbly idle, doing nothing better than following sport, eating and drinking too much, talking a lot, making great new-year resolutions and generally forgetting the rat-race of the previous year.

Most of the population picks up sticks for a few weeks and goes somewhere else. Perhaps to the bush or the shack at the beach, or to the city, or to the country cousin's farm. Wherever they go however, there is a grim determination that the holidays are here, and that nothing from any part of the outside world will intrude into these glorious days. That means that an already insular nation completely shuts out **all news** from overseas, and from trouble-spots around the globe. It also means that it is indifferent to the normal news of gloom and doom that the newspapers generally feed them, and instead it worries about what time the tide turns, and how we are going in the Davis Cup and the cricket.

The newspapers, cunning devils, know all this, and so they fill their few pages with lighter news and commentary and Letters, and give limited coverage to the bigger events that they would otherwise play up into big stories.

So this year, respectful as usual of the public's antipathy to any worrying news in January, they reported lazily on only a few matters. For example, a number of headlines appeared about **the problems in the Australian Labor**

**Party**. This body was having internal problems because it was under the control of the Trade Unions, and the more powerful of these were run by Communists. The Catholic Church was strongly opposed to Communism, and had by now organised its own faithful to do battle with the Reds.

So the scene was set for large confrontations in the future, and for a few weak headlines right now. But everything reported in January was old hat, the public had heard it all many times before, and simply wrapped Friday's fish in it.

Another situation that caught a few days of headlines was a growing dispute off the coast of China. You will probably remember that the Reds, led by Mao Tse Tung had finally gained control of China in 1949 by bloody revolution. In doing this, they had defeated the forces of the Nationalists, led by General Chiang Kai Shek. This latter General, with many supporters, had retreated to nearby islands and had set up his headquarters on Formosa. From there, he on the one hand, and the Reds on the other, had been conducting violent raids on each other's territory for a few years.

**Now**, the situation was bursting into the news with air raids of 200 planes bombing each other, and generally sticking their respective tongues out. There was obviously much trouble ahead in this region, because Mao wanted Formosa for the Reds, and he wanted the hopeless but annoying Chiang gone. Chiang for his part, was foolishly bragging that he would make a come-back, and re-conquer mainland China, always assuming the USA would back him up.

In the meantime, Oz was on hols, and only a little of this news filtered through. Later in the year, this might be important. But, right now, "We are not worried. We'll catch up with it later."

## STAGE SHOWS IN SYDNEY

Christmas and the New Year found the entertainment world alive with promise. There were tons of local shows, and a fair smattering of overseas productions. Children, of course, had a lot to choose from, but adults also had plenty. Add to that the number of good quality concerts of all types, and the Oz theatre was vibrant.

For example, the Empire Theatre had a "spectacular show for children, Direct from London." It was the pantomime, *Puss in Boots*, and provided world renouned skating stars and a galaxy of internationally famous speciality acts. This was presented as a matinee, and six hours later another show, *Rose Marie on Ice*, was said to be the first Australian musical comedy done on ice.

But, wait. If that is not enough ice for you, there is also *Cinderella on Ice* at the Palladium, and this has the added imprimatur that "Princess Margaret went to see it."

Apart from this Christmas fare, there was the dancing of the Borovansky Ballet, Peter Scriven Puppets were ready to keep you amused, England's singing sensation, David Hughes, supposedly "England's Heart Throb", was warbling away, and another Pom, Donald Peers, was selling his shmaltz at the Sydney Town Hall.

The movies were enthralling. How could you go past *Gone with the Wind*, on the great wide screen with the added enchantment of Perspecta Stereophonic Sound. Then there was *Brigadoon* with Gene Kelly. For those looking for comedy, Martin and Lewis were starring in whatever took their fancy, and at Wynyard you could enjoy continuous sessions showing a Three Stooges movie, two cartoons and three news reels.

For good measure, if you wanted to be more active, the Rathbone Academy of Dramatic Art would teach you to act, and Brian Blake would brush you up on the violin.

## ON HOLS? LETS GO FISHING

Seems like a good idea. Of course, you could use dynamite. **That was very popular at the time.** Suppose though that you are law-abiding and choose instead to use a rod and line. Then, without a shadow of a doubt, **your fish of choice would be trout.**

These fine fish were in many of the inland streams, and made a delectable meal. A few streams were being stocked each year by various authorities, and this was keeping their numbers up somewhat. There were however, some concerns that numbers were dwindling too fast.

**Letters, W Satchell.** To all those who have, in the past, experienced the thrills and the joys of trout fishing in our beautiful highland streams, the disappearance of trout must be a tragedy.

I blame the cormorant, but there may be other contributing causes. Whatever they are, something should be done to re-establish trout fishing as a holiday and tourist attraction.

Vigorous and systematic re-stocking, together with the wholesale destruction of cormorants would, in my opinion, completely replenish our streams within two or three years.

**Letters, W Bluett.** All the lovers of trout fishing will warmly commend Mr W Satchell for drawing public attention to the most unsatisfactory condition of our State's trout culture.

Over the past decade the position has become progressively worse. The Fisheries Department relies on restocking to cure all ills. But something far more comprehensive is needed than simply dumping additional fry from hatcheries into our rivers, a practice long since discredited in New Zealand, where trout culture is far more advanced than in Australia.

The accountancy records on the back of this season's licence are not going to solve the problem, no matter how closely followed by the errant fisherman. We want to know why it is that, for one takeable fish, a man has to land ten or more under the 12in limit.

I agree with Mr Satchell that the cormorant is responsible for much of the loss in big fish. The bird finds these an easier mark than the tiddlers. Last season quite 80 per cent of Rainbow, of 1lb and over, caught here (Goodradigbee) were scarred below the dorsal fin; probably they had depth of water in which they made their escape.

I am convinced from long observation that the trouble is far deeper seated than the obvious losses due to the coming and going of the voracious cormorant.

Trout have been established in NSW waters for over 70 years. The Fisheries Department must have kept tab on the propagation and culture of the fish over these long and changing years.

**Letters, P E Steindl.** W Bluett and most fishermen miss the main cause of the indifferent trout-fishing over the last few years.

The answer can be found in reports from all over New South Wales of drought conditions, off and on, for two years. These droughts were preceded by disastrous floods and, in fact, for three years most of our beautiful streams have been unsuitable for trout life.

Early this season, fish died by the thousand along the banks of the Goodradigbee. In January, 1954, I walked from the junction of the Cotter and Murrumbidgee to the Cotter dam wall; the banks were covered with hundreds of dead rainbow trout, from 2oz to 5lb. I have seen the same thing on many of our streams.

Two weeks ago I walked for a mile along the Murrumbidgee, which in a good season is one of the finest trout streams imaginable. Failing to "rise" a fish, I examined several pools overhung by willows, and in each trout were congregated in shoals of six to 20, ranging in size from 1lb to 4lb. They were in such a state of exhaustion that they could be pushed about with a rod.

These fish would probably not die, but they have little chance of evading "enemies." A good proportion will live to fight again, and when the seasons turn in favour of the trout we will enthuse in the delights of our streams until, once again, the seasons turn against us.

## PROBLEMS WITH PISTOL PACKING

**The 1956 Olympic Games were to be held in Melbourne next year.** With the all the fun and excitement that would come with those Games, however, **there would certainly be many problems**.

Just as one early example, Olympic pistol shooters were in the news. There is much talk about the problems raised by the guns being brought into Oz by the Olympic shooters. Would these people be allowed to have possession of their guns in our society where the free access to guns is restricted by law? Or should the guns be locked away until they were to be used?

It turned out that a decision was made that weapons would be held in the custody of the Olympic Committee and Police, and that they would be released to the shooters at appropriate times. It was obvious to all that this would become an administrative nightmare over the weeks of practice and competition.

But there were other objections. Forbes Carlyle started the ball rolling. He was prominent in the NSW Pentathlon Association at the time, and later became famous as the coach of many of our swimming champions.

He pointed out that "an Olympic pistol-shooter is a perfectionist to an extreme. He handles his pistol like a baby, and as regularly as the baby needs to come to its mother's breast, so the shooter needs to hold, caress his pistol, and practice, hour after hour, "dry" shooting. He does this in the privacy of his room at all hours of the day and night."

He, and others, pointed out the folly of competitors lining up each day to get their guns from Police authorities. They could see that overseas competitors would be most upset by this, and indeed that some might refuse to be so bullied.

Carlyle went on to attack the Games Organising Committee for not coming to terms long ago with all the problems that the Games will bring.

He anticipated that the cross-country horse events would have similar difficulties, and **he wondered whether Australia was civilised enough to take on the Olympic Games.**

## ALIGHTING FROM TRAMS

Often in the holiday period, the papers are flooded with Letters from writers who are quite happy to while away their time writing correspondence that might be considered trivial. This sequence below illustrates what a body of knowledge can be created when idle minds work together.

I should remind you that trams in those days had a stepping board right round them. To get off, you needed to take a step down from the body of the tram on to the stepping board, then take another step down onto the ground. Most people held onto a vertical rail that was placed near each exit to help you keep your balance.

**Letters, C Johnsen.** Only one woman in a thousand alights correctly from a tram.

There are three methods of leaving the footboard of a tram: Facing the driver; facing outwards; and facing to the rear. Of the three, only the first is correct. Should the tram move while one is alighting by either the second or third methods, she is liable to be spreadeagled on the roadway.

Possibly the psychologists could explain why women almost invariably alight the wrong way.

**Letters, R Morland.** It does not need a psychologist to tell us why women alight from a tram the wrong way.

A woman carries her handbag in her right hand. Therefore, she uses her left hand to grasp the left hand rail which turns her either out or around. Silly maybe but logical.

**Letters, M Green.** I am sure R Morland is wrong about women carrying their handbags in their right hands, except otherwise left-handed persons.

A picture in the SMH of January 6 shows the Duchess of Kent and her daughter with bags on their left hand wrists. A woman usually takes her purse or her bag with her right hand.

I have always carried a handbag in my left hand, and I do not think psychology would come into the matter.

**Letters, H M Eyre.** It is the usual practice for a woman to wait for a tram to stop before attempting to alight; then she steps off at right angles facing the road.

This practice might with advantage be followed by many men whose habit it is to jump off impatiently from moving vehicles.

**Letters, M H.** Could not the reason for a man's alighting correctly from a tram be that as a boy he learned to jump from a tram before it had stopped, whereas girls wait until the tram is stationary?

# THE PRICE OF FALSE TEETH

If you think that the above Letters were bordering on the trivial, then you were right. Now, however, we can raise a much more serious matter that stirred another lot of January minds into activity.

Over the last half-century the teeth of this nation have improved steadily. Most people would say that the main cause of this was the introduction of fluoride into drinking water, though there are still some, especially in Queensland, who deny that this was beneficial. In any case, false teeth back in 1955 were much more common than they are today, and became a hot topic when their cost was mentioned.

**Letters, Albert E Watts.** Brought to my notice recently in the "Herald" was the stated cost of artificial teeth, namely 40 Pounds.

May I mention, as a dental mechanic who worked in the West End of London, that a complete set of teeth could be then made, at a profit, for 2 Pounds.

Having made dentures for many eminent and public persons, including Peers of the Realm, I consider a well-made and artistic set of teeth, enabling the owner to masticate food as nature intended, could now be made in vulcanite or plastic material at a cost not exceeding 5 Pounds.

Any intelligent girl could be taught the necessary skill and technical knowledge in three months as to the preparation and manufacture of a set of well-fitting dentures.

**Letters, Audrey Hughes.** Mr Alfred E Watts is, I believe, living in the past.

On present-day prices, it is impossible to make a set of teeth for 5 Pounds, unless they are made at a loss. The cost of English teeth from the dental depot is 3 Pounds 15/4 alone, and added to that are the dental materials used, time and labour in the surgery taking impressions, bite and try in, and also the mechanic's wages.

In any suburb today you may purchase a full set of teeth, inclusive of extractions, for from 20 to 30 guineas.

**Letters, G H B A.** May I applaud the letter of Albert E Watts, on the cost of false teeth?

A relative (a fully qualified dentist with a large practice) tells me that the best sets of false teeth cost him less than 7 Pounds 10 shillings, but admits that he charges from 20 Pounds to 45 Pounds, according to his judgment of the ability of the client to pay.

Similarly, in the optician business, best quality lenses are sold by wholesalers at less than 30/ a dozen. Yet, on inquiring from six opticians in Sydney, I was quoted prices from 4 Pounds 15 shilling to 6 Pounds 6 shillings to put two new lenses into my own frame.

**Comment.** It should be remembered that the dentist had a big hand in the production of the teeth. That is, he measured the teeth, and fitted them for a technician to make. It was illegal for a customer to go directly to a dental technician. This added an extra layer of cost.

## WHAT ABOUT FLUORIDATION?

This was another hot topic. Should local Councils exercise their right to fluoridate water supplies? This was still a matter for debate. At the slightest prompting, the anti-fluoridation lobby was at the ready to push its views.

**Letters, Ernest Mende.** Many will feel obliged to you for publishing on January 29 a cable from London about the negative sides of the plan to add fluorine to drinking water.

Generations of Britons, Australians and others had excellent teeth, although there were not subject to compulsory intake of fluorine. Supposing those children, who alone can possibly benefit from fluorine, would make even 20 per cent of the population, why should the other 80 per cent be compelled to take adulterated water that admittedly cannot benefit, but may harm, them?

**Letters, S J P Crago.** Fluorine fanatics are agitating for the chance to interfere with our water supplies.

In all the controversy over this matter, one very important point has been overlooked, namely, that fluorination, in the long run, gets out of hand and cannot be controlled. For that reason, some of the American cities which came early into the field of fluorination have now abandoned it; it was found to be cumulative and dangerous in its effects.

Stock consume the fluorine; garden produce contains it; beer becomes impregnated with it; it gets into soft drink, milk shakes and ice cream and into practically every article of food.

**Comment.** I don't know whether it was the war-time lack of toothpaste and brushes, **or** whether it was ignorance of dental hygiene, **or** whether that there was no dentist within cooee, but the children in my village, when I was at primary school, all had rotten teeth. Despite the above, I suspect that fluoride would have helped a lot.

## DOG MATTERS

**Letters, Dog Lover.** The following is an old bush remedy for tick poisoning with which I have saved the lives of dogs and cats, even when gone in the hind legs. Take a handful of brown stems of ordinary bracken fern. Boil in one pint of water till reduced to half. Cool and give a tablespoon to animal every two hours. It will vomit the poison. Then give strengthening food such as egg flips and a little weak brandy.

**Another Letter** from a reader called Another Dog Lover was very long and confused. However, when translated, it said that "I have dogs and I love them. My dogs do not get ticks, so I could not try out your remedy on them. But I love egg flips, and I love brandy. So I had a lot of both for myself, and waited for the effect. Nothing happened.

"So I had some more. Still no result. So I made the brandy stronger. I kept doing this for a while. Then I got a great result. I vomited as you forecast.

"So I can verify that at least part of your remedy works, Good advice, Thank you."

## FEBRUARY NEWS ITEMS

Some of you will remember **leaving a jug out on the front verandah** each night, so that the milk man could fill it with milk. **This was so-called raw milk.** Now in the major metropolitan areas of NSW, **raw milk is to be replaced by bottled milk**....

The milko will **still deliver this milk, and will collect the empties**. The change is being made for health reasons, and the price will rise by one halfpenny up to 11 pence for a pint. Customers should rinse, but not clean, the bottles.

February 3rd. **Bad, bad news**. England won the fourth cricket Test Match against Australia in Adelaide yesterday. This means that they **retained the Ashes**, and Poms can gloat for another few years.

A swimmer was killed by a shark off a small beach in Sydney Harbour last weekend. A well-known philanthropist, Sir Edwards Hallstrom has chosen seven large sports-fishing vessels, and agreed with their skippers that **if any of them capture and kill this shark this weekend then he will pay that skipper 1,000 Pounds**....

**Will it be the killer shark?** To find out, each shark will be **slit down the gut, and its stomach contents examined**. If there are body parts there, then that will be a suspect shark. **If there is more than one suspect shark**, the body parts will be examined in more detail until the correct one is identified....

**Post Script**. The **game-boats** went out in force, but **were unsuccessful**.

Britain has announced that it has the capacity to make a **hydrogen bomb**. The Australian Minister for Supply was quick to say that **such a bomb would not be tested in Australia**. This statement was necessary because, **in the past** on several occasions, Australia had agreed to **Britain using Australia for the testing of its atom bombs**.

**Huge flooding occurred at Maitland and Singleton** in NSW's Hunter Valley. At Maitland, **15,000 of its 23,000 residents were homeless**. Two men were drowned when two houses were swept away in Maitland. Two soldiers fell off a truck into raging waters, and are missing believed drowned....

**Two men in a railway signal box** were rescued by a helicopter. **They fell from the rope, onto electric wires, and were electrocuted. The helicopter crashed. Four other men in the signal box were drowned when the box was washed away. Sixteen people were drowned in one day. Forty two were drowned over a week.**

**A five-foot goanna caused panic in the main street** of Gosford, in regional NSW. It ran into a barber's shop, and the customers ran out. It then bolted 100 yards along the footpath, tongue spitting. Dozens of women screamed. It ran back again, until **a man battered it to death with a piece of wood, and hung it over a fence....**

**This was clearly a warning to all Oz goannas to stay out of the main street of Gosford.**

# THE EVILS OF THE DEMON DRINK

The **new** liquor laws in NSW were now in force. The major provision was that the pubs had to close at 6.30 pm on weekdays and Saturdays, but were to re-open again at 7.30, and stay open until 10 pm. The idea behind this was to redirect the six-o'clock swillers home for an evening meal, with the hope that if they did come out again, they would be more civilised.

In the first week, the city pubs were almost empty after dinner, and stayed that way for the next week. The suburbs and country towns were very busy in the first week, but when the novelty wore off, they were only half full in the second week.

It seemed though that opposition to the new laws had gone underground, with the realisation that there was no way of having the laws changed back to their previous form. So Letters changed to new issues. One issue was dress codes.

Previously, **night clubs** had always insisted on a dress code that, for example, insisted that men wore ties. A few snooty city pubs also demanded this, often only after dark. But now, local pubs were opening up lounges, and forgetting that they were still locals.

**Letters, D Burrows.** Now that liquor reform is an established fact, surely it is not too much to hope for sanity in other directions.

On the first night of "civilised" drinking, it was warm and humid. I was dressed to suit the conditions in well-cut trousers, belt, a clean white, long-sleeved shirt, and brown tie.

This attire brought forth an objection from the drink waiter of a hotel. It seems that the rule of the house, not a first-rate one, incidentally, declared that in order to enjoy a drink in the lounge, **men must wear a jacket**.

It is high time the perspiring male revolted against such arbitrary pronouncements.

**Comment.** This battle over dress codes for drinkers was fought for the next decade. Hoteliers who wanted to be regarded as having a high class establishment demanded ties or jackets for men. It is doubtful that they achieved their objectives of reaching a higher class.        .

Another problem was the extra noise.  Some of this was pub traffic, but pub-owners were quick to bring singers and bands into their beer gardens, especially at the weekends, to stamp out any chance of conversation.  During the week, they played recorded music at full bore. Did you drink more if you could not hear people talk?  I can think of no other reason for the extra decibels. Still, here's what a few other people thought about noise.

**Letters, W R.**  We are among the unfortunates who live adjacent to a suburban hotel.

Needless to say, we voted for 6 p.m. closing as the Saturday beer garden revels for a few months previously had given us a foretaste of 10 p.m. closing.

Our apprehensions have proved only too well founded. Each night we have canned music amplified to a degree which shows the beer patrons are so insensible to noise that the music also reaches residents two or three blocks away.  Our own radio fails to drown the horrible din next door, and it is useless to speak from one room to another.

Do **drinkers** demand such entertainment, or is it an expression of the hotelkeeper's glee?

**Letters, J S Watson.** Your correspondent, W R, is fortunate indeed if he is troubled only by beer garden noises; after all, these must cease about 10 p.m.

In four years' residence in built-up areas of Sydney, I have come to the conclusion that the average Australian is never happy unless he is making loud noises by radio, gramophone or mouth for at least 18 hours every day.

Furthermore, there is no means of combating a noise nuisance. Driven recently by a 2 a.m. radio-fan, into inquiring what official action I could take, I was amazed to find that the police are powerless; only the health inspector of the local authority is able to take any action, and his powers are hedged and restricted, and dependent on all kinds of conditions, so as to make complaints futile.

I would add that I have lived in several other cities both in Australia and abroad and in only one can I recall a similar volume of noise – in Naples.  There at least the musical taste was superior.

The question raised by the obvious success of extended drinking hours also raised the question of Sunday opening.

**Letters, M Tolhurst.**  Now that 10 p.m. closing has proved itself workable and pleasant, who is for Sunday opening as well, as in England?

This would be an additional social boon and would help to rid our Sabbath of its social gloom.  I venture to say – in anticipation of the usual protests when anyone suggests brighter Sundays – that more people would turn out to church if they could enjoy a convivial glass after service.  Motorists, by burning a couple of gallons of petrol, can get a drink on Sundays.  Why not everyone who wants it?

**Comment.** Some of you will remember the rule that said motorists who travelled 20 miles would doubtless be thirsty. So, if they did this on a Sunday, they could call in at any local pub or (now) the beer garden, 20 miles from home, and drink as much as they liked. So, many motorists took off on Sunday morning, drove their 20 miles to a nice country pub, and had a day on the grog. Needless to say, they then drove home.

I feel that **nowadays** this would be seen as objectionable for some reason. Maybe you can work out why.

**Letters, B R Lugg.** In England the public house is a national institution, playing a valuable part in the life of the community.

With liberal laws and good administration, the same could apply in Australia; puritanical legislation leads to intolerance.

Australians are waking up to this, and demanding that at least they be permitted to enjoy the same freedom as exists in England.

**Letters, G C L.** So now someone wants a Sunday swill as well; and the sly argument is that more people will go to worship if afterwards they can rush to a pub and drink. What next? It seems clear to me that liquor drinkers are like spoiled children; the more freedom they gain to indulge themselves, the more they crave. If it is true that hotel bars are open in England on Sundays, it is a shameful state of affairs. Voters would surely never countenance that here.

**Letters, G Preston.** Now that we have 10 p.m. closing, there does not appear to be any reason why Sunday trading should not be introduced. It would be a popular innovation.

We should infuse vitality into our dull Sabbath and provide amusement where and when it is most needed.

**Letters, Whole-Hoger.** One of your writers, advocating the opening of hotels on Sunday, suggested that church attendances would be improved if the members of the congregation could relax after the sermon over a few beers at the local water-hole.

Why not go one better and **establish a well-stocked bar in the vestry**, thus rendering a service to the church-going public and at the same time providing a boost to the parish revenue? Beer is, in the view of many Australians, the most important thing in life; so why not use it as an adjunct to religious observance – or religious observance as an adjunct to beer, if that order is preferred?

**Letters, A C Ward.** Assuming that M Tolhurst's prescription of after-service drinking in legally opened hotels as one way of dispelling "social gloom" on Sundays is seriously presented, may I have the privilege of offering something more certain and satisfactory – visits to those who are incapacitated and lonely, with friendship's warmth and cheering word. Sunday is never too long or "gloomy" to those who use its free hours in that manner.

**Letters, CV.** Those correspondents who seem appalled by the suggestion that beer gardens be opened on Sundays are woefully illogical in their attitude. Restaurants, tea-rooms, and milk bars are open on the Sabbath, and inasmuch as alcoholic refreshment is an accepted amenity, why should it not be available then, too? After all, if "the better the day the better the deed," surely the better the day the more pleasant the drink.

**Comment.** NSW politicians had taken a big risk in extending trading hours, because some of the churches were very much opposed to the new laws. At the moment, **Sunday trading was a step too far for these politicians**. You will notice that, in the above Letters, there were **none**

**from the Churches or clergymen**. This group were never reticent in expressing their views, so it must have been obvious to them that there was no immediate threat.

Still, there was an element that was not daunted by reality, and **its** voice **was** heard in the above collection.

## AGE PENSION: WHAT'S CHANGED?

This Letter by an Age Pensioner will ring a bell with many readers.

**Letters, D A.**  By decent living, thrift, self-denial, and working for more than 60 years, I have managed to save 2,500 Pounds, including the proceeds of a life assurance policy payable at 60.  Most of this amount consists of Government bonds bearing interest at a fraction over 3 per cent.

Some of my children are buying homes for themselves, and I would like very much to help them.  Being over 80, with failing sight, and no longer able to work, I might reasonably expect to be entitled to some benefit under the Old Age Pensions Act, but I find I am not eligible because I have more than 1,750 Pounds.

If I gave financial help to my children, thus reducing my capital to 1,750 Pounds, I would thereby disqualify myself for a pension.  That is the legal position.

For some time, I have been drawing on capital, and every day brings me nearer the time when I will have to convert my bonds into cash.

I contend that I have a natural and moral right to do as I wish with what is my own, for the help and comfort of my children, without being penalised.

The Government says: "No, you have not.  You can divest yourself of your capital in any other way you wish; by gambling on the racecourse, or squandering it in other ways, and you will be able to get the pension;

but, **if you do it to help your children**, we will see that you suffer for it by denying you every benefit to which, by reason of age and good character, you would, otherwise, be entitled." That is how the present law operates.

I regard such a law as so unjust as to be immoral in the sight of God. While I am compelled to submit to it, I deny any moral obligation to obey it.

**Letters, E Martin Baker.** Your very excellent leader on the threat of inflation should be taken to heart by every man and woman interested in national or personal welfare.

Its conclusion, that "means must be found of encouraging personal savings," and that "income saved within the country is the best and safest means of financing national development," is so obviously true as to defy contradiction.

In the next column but one appears a letter from an aged correspondent who, because he has practised this personal saving all his life, is denied all vestige of the pension enjoyed by those who have never saved at all. Here is a striking negation of the principle you so ably and accurately enunciate.

Why would such a man save and be sensible all his life, and yet be denied a pension? If there is any justice, he would get the pension, and the wastrels would get none. After all, it is **his** money being given away.

**Letters, T Moyles.** Your correspondent DB knows little of finance and government. He apparently does not know that the Government takes our money for fifty years and then gives it to someone else. It will do the same to those "who are now doing the work to keep this country going."

A pension should be like any loan. You lend it to the Government, and it gives it back when it is needed.

But it should be given back to the people who made the loan in the first place, and not to those who did not.

**Comment.** It is remarkable that so little has changed for pensions in the last 60 years. Even the arguments are still the same.

## A MOTHERS QUESTION

A mother asked the following question.

**Letters, Puzzled Parent.** Having completed all but two years of a part-time degree course at the University of Technology, my son now tells me that he is "giving it away."

His reasons are two. In his words, the last straw is the 100 p.c. increase in fees which is to operate this year, and the other the possibility of total war.

After listening politely to my argument that Australia needs technical men of specialised training, and that there should be a future ahead of him satisfactory in the fulfilment of his ambitions as well as giving him financial security, my son suggested that I should read the advertisement section of the newspaper "Positions Vacant."

He pointed out that in the commercial sphere, he can immediately receive an additional 250 Pounds a year in salary, and that the future is so uncertain because of the **possibility of wholesale use of atom and hydrogen bombs**, he is not going to bother about it, but instead do all those things he has foregone whilst studying four or five nights a week, such as attending concerts and so on.

He finally reminded me that I had lost my father in the 1914-18 war and my husband in the last war. Just where, he asked, had either man benefited Australia in their professions which they had followed for only a tragically short time.

What is the answer I should give my son?

Half a dozen people had their responses published. They did not dwell long on the question of the cost education question. They all shrugged it off. One writer said that fees had not been increased since before the war, and so a rise now was to be expected. Another said that it was "a domestic issue", and another said the cost of education reflected "the economic realities of the times". Not much wisdom there.

The second question produced more serious discussion.

**Letters, Ralph Reader.** The real point is whether the satisfaction that comes from a life where one's work is at the same time one's interest and pleasure is sufficient to justify the long period of study, the forfeit of so much spare time, the limitation of recreation and pleasure, the financial sacrifice and at the end of it all an income less than the man (perhaps in commerce) who took the easier way.

The unambitious life can lead him to happiness depending on the wise use of leisure and, if he is lucky, money. On the other hand let him be in no doubt as to the rewards for toil and study.

Throughout his entire life he will find the days too short, there will be no place for boredom, no sense of daily grind. There will be stimulation and interest, problems and the thrills of solving them.

Satisfaction in this life does not come so much from the achievement of one's goal as from the striving for it. The study period with all its tribulations has its own reward.

**Letters, Quartus.** The real question is "What shall I get?" then obviously he is one with the vast majority of individuals and nations. That is the real crux of our problem. Study is its own reward, and a youth of Australia in the twentieth century, is no wiser than a Roman citizen of the first century, unless that is perceived. A laborer can have economic security without understanding a technical or human problem.

Many of us lost loved ones in the two world wars, but that sad fact does not relieve us of the responsibility to future generations. Security, either physical or economic, is not to be compared with the adventure of putting all we can into life, and our times are surely ripe for disinterested service.

**Letters, Graduate.**  If this lad has read the record of road deaths this year, how is he ever going to face the traffic to tackle his commercial job?  If he has ever read about criminal assaults, can he ever overcome fear of leaving his home?

As to the menace of war, he must know that this threat has hung over men since time immemorial. The fact that his grandfather and father lost their lives through war is purely accidental. The possibility that he will survive a holocaust is strong enough to be reckoned with.

He should strive for the highest possible standard of knowledge, skill, and experience in his technical profession, provided he is really interested in the subjects he has chosen.  His greatest reward will, then, be the satisfaction of achievement.

It is up to him to pull his weight and not to seek, as he appears to do, merely an easy life and easy money.

**Personal comment.** The middle class in Australia strongly supported the concept of education. All the above writers were readers of the *SMH* that catered to the middle class, and were clearly of the opinion that Little Johnny should keep on with his studies.

At the time, the working class outnumbered the middle class. Of course, in Australia, there was nothing like the "Class System" that still persisted in Britain, but here there was still a divide that was apparent. So I raise the question: **did the working class espouse higher education?**

**I have come to the conclusion that I do not know the answer to that.** I have a lot of evidence to say that it did give it great support. This comes from my own and my acquaintances' experience.  It also comes for the impressions I have gained in doing my research for these books. So many times I have seen and heard parents say, in effect, that the only way out of some situation for the children was to get a good education and then a good job. Many of them also valued it because they realised that to live in ignorance, or some variety of it, was to miss many of the real joys of life

Yet on the other hand, I have heard an equal number of scoffers among the working classes. One prevalent attitude was that **the children did not need education.**  After all, so-and-so left school at thirteen years of age, and went on to become a such-and-such. Davie Smith couldn't put two and two together, yet he's got the best house in this town. Bob Hunter got his Leaving Certificate, went to University, and won't even look at us now.

So did those of the working classes support education and higher education?  My answer, for what it is worth, is that **some did, and others did not.**  What do you think?

**Some sixty year later,** the question is purely academic. At the moment, if you want of a decent job, you need some sort of education. This is true not only in the professions, such as medicine, law, engineering, and pharmacy.

You need tickets, and diplomas to get most jobs, and then to advance further up the career ladder. Some of these are just certification courses that say you can operate a certain machine, others are serious long-term training such as for nursing and teaching. Most of them however do need some form of education, and the days of successful Old Mick, who could not spell his own name, are long gone.

## A MEMORY TEST: MEDICAL MATTERS

Do you remember **Scotts Emulsion**? **Bonninngtons Irish Moss**, and its petrel oxymel of carrigeen? **Cornwells extract of malt?**

Which pain-reliever did you use? **Aspro, Bex or APC.** There were not many alternatives available.

Did you get a monthly **dose of parafin oil**? Or even more interesting, **castor oil?**

Did your parents have **painful ulcers,** wrongly thought to be caused by worrying?

## NEWS AND VIEWS

An Australian patrol in New Guinea has found **a tribe that has never before seen a white man**. It is at the top of the Fly River, and has about 20,000 people in it.

**The Queen has given approval** for an annual race at Randwick Racecourse to be called "**the Queen Elizabeth Stakes**". It will carry prize-money of 8,000 Pounds.

# MARCH NEWS ITEMS

Oh goody. **The Brits have announced that they have started manufacture of the hydrogen bomb.** Sleep well, in the knowledge that the US and Russia already have stockpiles....

France announced a week later that it **too will soon manufacture hydrogen bombs.**

The Federation of American Scientists suggested to the United Nations that controls be placed on atom bomb testing **to safeguard the human race.**

**The flood of US performers continues.** The latest arrival was **Johnny Ray**. He was greeted by 10,000 screaming teenagers, **who did all the normal things**, like tearing his clothes, breaking windows and doors, and knocking him down. It was enough to make you **CRY....**

At the other end of the spectrum, tickets started to sell for the **ABC Youth Concert Series** for the year. **A queue started to develop 26 hours before sales began**, and grew substantially since. The concerts will be given by the **Sydney Symphony Orchestra and others of renown**. The concerts were for patrons **under 25 years of age....**

Though in case you get the impression that high culture is at last beating off the popular rabble, American nutcase band-leader, **Spike Jones**, got the hero's welcome a week later at Sydney Airport. **Question:** Who was`the winner? **Answer:** *Beedle-bum*?

**Indian High Commissioner**, General Cariappa, was driving past **the War Memorial at Gundagai**. He stopped and he and members of staff **used sickles to slash the high grass surrounding the Memorial**, and threw away empty beer bottles and cigarette packets which lay inside the Memorial….

**He washed the memorial tablet until its inscription stood out clearly**. He saluted the Memorial, then entered the diplomatic car and drove off. He said later he wanted to paint the nearby fences, but the shops were shut. He had done this type of cleaning up at many other locations in Australia….

A wicked Letter-writer said that what **Australia needed was more Indian High Commissioners.**

**The Menzies Government had been in power for five years. The Labor Party was in never-ending turmoil**, with factional fighting and threatened break-away always on the cards. Many people were saying that the two principal Labor politicians were a hindrance to the Party, and that it **would never win an election while either of them was Leader. These were Doc Evatt, and Arthur Calwell….**

At the end of March, **the Labor Party had been on the front page of the *SMH* every day for a fortnight**. These were not good-news stories, but rather they spoke of **bitter fighting at the National and at the State level**. There`was no hope that Labor would gain office while it continued down the path of self-destruction.

# HUNTER VALLEY FLOODS

Everyone was talking about the floods in Maitland, Singleton and beyond. Even today, 60 years later, some oldies still use these floods as a yardstick to measure anything subsequent. There were too many deaths. The damage to housing, properties and infrastructure was immense. Social and community life in the aftermath was disrupted for months.

**Personal Memories.** I was caught up in the flood in two ways. **Firstly**, I was brought up in a small coal-mining town called Abermain, in the Cessnock region. This town, while not affected by flooding, was completely isolated for three weeks, so an outsider like me could not visit my birth-place.

**Secondly**, I happened to be in Singleton at the time. Not by choice, rather by draft. That is, over the previous two years I had finished my basic training in the National Service (in the Army), and was in Singleton for the last of my three follow-up annual camps. I was scheduled to spend three weeks there, with a thousand other reluctant warriors.

As it turned out, we were happy in a way to find that we did not have a single parade. Nor did we fire a single rifle, nor bayonet a single scarecrow, nor dig a single trench. Instead, we were put on trucks each morning, and slowly ferried through the low-lying floodwaters into the country-city of Singleton.

We then hopped down, often up to our knees in water, and cleaned the mess out of streets, and houses, and public buildings. We all felt that this work was well worth doing, and we **did** work hard. We kept this up every day for three weeks, and then were replaced by the next batch of Nashos. By the time we had finished, you could scarcely see where we had been, so big was the overall task.

## THE REACTION TO THE FLOODS

Almost every city in the nation set up a fund to gather donations for the victims, and were well supported by their communities. At the same time, newspapers carried Letters that initially spoke about the suffering from the loss of life and property, and then came down to **longer-term considerations**. It is these latter that I will focus on.

**Letters, V P Turner.**  In these days when heavy earth-moving equipment is available, it seems pathetic and appalling that the populations of unprepared towns in the path of the floods are turning out with sandbags and shovels.

I write from recent personal observation of miles of the remains of these so-called levees, during surveys around the back of various towns.  The remains of these levees reveal that near the top, where the break-throughs start, they are very thin and makeshift.

What is needed to prevent this repeated loss of life and property is a properly constructed bank.  No matter how big the town, or flood, using reasonable tolerance it would be comparatively easy to prepare for the water that might come next year, or at any time in the next 50 years.

**Letters, M W Wilkinson.**  Mr V P Turner's ideas about levees are, I fear, not the remedy for overflowing rivers.

All our slow-flowing rivers have for many years been **silting up** at the expense of fertile lands, **thus raising the river bottoms closer to the level of their natural banks** and simultaneously adding to the risk of overflow.

This is, of course, allied to erosion of land, perhaps many miles distant.

The Government and owners are doing much to stop gradually such erosion, but the rivers badly need desilting. **To raise their banks would merely build toward a greater disaster** from an elevated river in the future. The silt, which is valuable soil, should be put to good use.

A few days later, attention turned to bigger-scale prevention. There were many ideas offered, and foremost of these was the call for **more dams**. One writer said that the use of **local** construction firms finished up in costing far too much, and also in taking too long to build. He advocated that large national firms be used, with their huge range of equipment. "This might not please the locals, because they want years of work out of a job. But it will get the job done in a reasonable time, and at a price the nation can afford."

Other Letters added to the array.

**Letters, Irrawaddy.** Dams to control river flooding must always be expensive, long-term projects if works of this kind are anything to go by in New South Wales.

There is a simpler way. If the nozzle of the garden hose is closed and the tap is turned on, the hose will burst. That, in effect, is what has been happening in the Hunter Valley since extended cultivation allowed vast quantities of silt to be washed off into the river and almost block its exit.

With several miles now silted up until nothing but light draught craft can use the river, the blockage in the hose is almost complete.

From Maitland down to Newcastle there is enough silt to lift the level of the Hexham swamps, and adjacent lowlands, several feet above present levels. The whole of this silt handled by suction dredging plant, could be pumped in liquid form to flow all over the low-lying margins of the Hunter River.

At the same time, as the silt is spread, the bed of the river is opened, and between the two useful processes, flood mitigation is under way at a far cheaper rate than any dam.

There is no doubt about it. If Port Hunter is to remain a first-class port, extensive dredging as described will have to be carried out **all day and every day** for some considerable time before the river bed is once more wide and deep enough to carry the flood volumes.

Levees composed of dry silt will be far more effective than sandbags, for they can be extensive enough to carry higher-level roads, as the bunds do in India and Burma.

Suction dredging and pumping are the cheapest, easiest and best for present urgent purposes. The silt, and the spaces to take it, are there right on the spot, all ready for quick action.

At a later stage, tributes came in to acknowledge the relief efforts of various volunteers.

**Letters, A Cessnock Medical Practitioner.** On Sunday morning, February 27, an appeal was broadcast in Cessnock for 1,000 men to go to Singleton and assist in the clearing of the town.

Within an hour there were 1,500 offering to go. On Monday, 2,000 men went to Singleton, and on Tuesday 2,500 offered their services. No worker received a penny of remuneration from any source.

The restoration of the water and electricity supplies of Singleton was accomplished entirely by the efforts of Cessnock engineers and their employees. In the course of this work, mineworkers cheerfully manhandled heavy equipment through mud, water, and flood debris to help restore these essential services. Their work was highly commended by the engineer in charge.

Centres for the distribution of food and clothing have been established. The clergy of Cessnock have done a magnificent job in this regard, ably assisted by the local Red Cross, Rotary and Lions Clubs. During the day of the worst crisis, Cessnock bakers baked continuously.

The women of Cessnock organised round-the-clock canteen services at several points in the stricken areas and are deserving of the highest praise.

On March 3, it was stated over the air that Cessnock was using too much water. I would like to say that much of this water was being used by the women of Cessnock in their own homes and their own washing machines – washing clothing for people in floodbound Singleton and Maitland.

Miners' lodges have donated from their own funds several thousands of pounds. I have been unable to obtain an exact figure, though I believe that one lodge alone gave 1,200 Pounds. Mining companies in the north have not only freely lent, but have also delivered to sites where it was needed, electrical and pumping equipment.

Tradesmen of all classes from Cessnock, Weston, Abermain and Kurri Kurri deserve special mention for their untiring efforts freely given, and their skill and ingenuity exhibited in the most adverse possible circumstances.

These are but some of the activities going on behind the general scene in these mining towns, and they should not go unacknowledged. They are unspectacular activities, but are none the less worthy of public notice.

Tributes came in for other groups, including the wharfies where large numbers also assisted mightily, without pay.

As flood-relief money became available, the method of allocating came under scrutiny. The following Letter raised a good point.

> **Letters, J Brown.** Is the proposed method of distributing flood relief in the best interests of the flood victims? Have they been consulted or given a chance to point out past defects in the system?
>
> Reports from earlier floods condemn the inclusion of "locals" on committees, whether they are aldermen, police or businessmen. Their function on the committee entitles them to know the financial position of every person applying for relief, but **no person in a small country town will divulge this personal information**.
>
> Hundreds of desperate people who were ruined financially in past floods would not apply for relief because their pride and dignity would not allow them to tell these local nabobs that they "did not have a cracker." This is no snobbish outlook. Laborers on the basic wage would not apply even though their plight was obvious.
>
> Apparently this unsuitable system was planned by city-ites who have no notion of small town life.
>
> Cannot a panel of magistrates be appointed to distribute the funds through private interviews with applicants, assisted by clerks and experts from the cities? Branch managers of banks are the only locals to whom the victims will confide their private affairs. Any other locals on these committees are a drawback to fair distribution.

Then a lady popped up with a suggestion that at first glance seemed light-weight but, on reflection, was very sensible.

**Letters, Alice W O'Sullivan.** While the tragedy of the recent floods is still fresh in mind and such a magnificent response is being made to the various funds, may I suggest that we each give something from our own homes: kitchenware, china, linen, a pair of curtains – even a vase or a picture: anything to help remake a home quickly.

I feel this idea will appeal to housewives and be of real assistance. Perhaps receiving depots would indicate their willingness to accept household items, now that clothes and blankets are not urgently required.

I have doubts, though, about whether the above proposal is practical.

Then, to finish off the flood, this final Letter.

**Letters, D Dyson, District Office, Madang, New Guinea.** I enclose a letter I received with 25 Pounds for the NSW Flood Relief Fund. Quite a few villages have given donations to the fund, this particular one with a written letter, which is unusual. Here is the letter, together with a rather free translation of the pidgin used.

Nemba Won Iap, - Mifela Lotman bilong Begesin e laik salim moni bilong helpim ol man meri bilong Australia samting bilong ol I lus long warer. Em Tasal.

Mi Taisaip, Headman. Begesin, March 19.

**Translation:-** District Commissioner, We all, men from Bagasin, we like to give money to help all man woman from Australia something belonging to all they lose in the water. That is all.

Mi Taisaip, Headman. Bagasin, March 19.

**A personal comment.** Over the years of writing these books, I have seen many floods come and go. Everyone who lives through a flood (or a bushfire) thinks it is the worst ever, so I need to be careful when I say that the Hunter floods throughout the early 1950's were among that worst-ever category. But I can speak with the backing of hundreds of people who I talk to in writing these books, and they too earmark the Maitland floods at that time as being special.

In any case, there are lots of authorities that tell me that such events will never occur again. **To be brief, I do not believe them.** They talk about levee walls being higher, about dredging the rivers, about planting trees. I am not convinced. These mitigation measures will, I fear, offer no resistance to the vast torrents of water that I saw in 1955.

**Still, I have been wrong before.** Maybe the experts know more that I do. I hope so.

## BATTERY HENS

The chook industry was very immature by today's standards, and consisted of about three big operators in the eastern States, hundreds of farmers growing hens in largish sheds as a sideline, and thousands of people in towns and suburbs running chooks in their backyards to produce enough eggs for the family.

These latter growers were not licensed, but were **regulated, and policed regularly**. The restraints on them varied from State to State, and from time to time, but generally they were allowed 18 hens and chickens, and a few roosters above that.

Inspectors would spring surprise visits on these growers, and issue fines to anyone exceeding the limits. The inspectors also checked for grossly bad feeding and watering practises, and that sheds offered suitable protection from the weather.

The bigger production units were given similar inspections, and overall it can be said that the mass of hens were saved from the most unsavoury conditions.

Now, however, the larger producers were learning new tricks from Britain and the US. The big innovation was the **introduction of battery-hen techniques**.

Variations occurred all over the place, but generally hens were kept inside most of the time, in very close proximity to each other, and were not given roosts to sleep on. It seemed to many that this was a most unnatural way for them to live, and objections and discussions were plentiful and often impassioned.

**Letters, V Farrell.** Recently, much publicity has been given to cruelty, in different forms, to animals. While some positive action has been taken in the method of handling stock and the use of the live hare, I feel some attention should be given to the battery method of egg production.

This method of keeping a fowl cooped in a small cage, with only a wire perch and not enough room to move or stretch, let alone exercise its body or wings, is profound cruelty of another age – almost barbaric.

It is inconceivable to me how people can bring themselves to earn their living at such extreme cruelty to a bird.

The fowl does a noble job in providing us with a very nutritious food. Should it be subjected to such shocking treatment?

BIRD LOVER of Sydney agreed, and said it was "the most barbarous thing I have come across for some time, and quite **unworthy of a Christian community**".

**Letters, P G Mason.** I read with surprise letters critical of "battery" poultry keeping.

Figures and information supplied by the Department of Agriculture prove beyond doubt that fowls kept in cages are not subject to cruelty. If a bird or animal is treated cruelly certain conditions will result, such as loss of appetite, wasting, flesh blemishes, nausea and generally a marked decline in activity.

Figures available indicate that fowls kept in cages produce as many or more eggs in comparison with other methods. The birds increase in weight consistently, they remain tender and they eat and drink readily. Each bird receives a balanced vitaminised ration of food plus clean water, and is virtually free from parasitic infestation.

**Letters, Mrs J Gee.** There is almost no smell from the battery, the cages are always clean and in wet weather cause no discomfort. The birds are placid and contented and eggs are clean and easily collected. The high cost of the cages is the worst drawback.

**Letters, S A Wakefield.** Horror of "battery" poultry farming has often been expressed in Britain, where 60 per cent of total egg production is said to come from caged birds.

Critics usually do not take into consideration that in the matter of shelter, feeding, protection from natural enemies and from bullying from its own kind, **the caged bird may be living in luxury**, and is often happier and healthier than in a flock on the ground.

The close confinement (which in a well-designed cage does allow the bird to move and stretch though not to flap its wings) may not be as cruel to the caged bird as it seems to human beings who project themselves in to the same situation.

**Letters, (Mrs) K M Raymond.** With regard to this barbarous practice, the RSPCA in London has had the following to say:-

"Consider the life of hens imprisoned permanently in small wire cages just large enough to hold them, deprived forever of their freedom and all chance of healthy exercise. These little prisons were not devised primarily for the well-being of their occupants but for their commercial exploitation to convert them into egg-laying machines.

The birds are deprived of their natural habit of scratching for food, which keeps them healthy, and are doomed to spend their days in unnatural inactivity, with no comfort of a dusty earth bath, no raking in deep leaves for hidden titbits, no preening in the sun, no going to roost with others on a comfortable perch when evening falls. Just a wire floor on which to crouch down, solitary, to sleep.

This is their thwarted existence until such time as the jailer receives insufficient eggs, when they are ruthlessly culled."

**Letters, Addled.** As a small backyard user of the battery method of keeping hens, I feel sure that we aren't as cruel as we appear to be.

We have five children, and a dozen hens which have completely kept us in eggs over the last 12 months.

The elder children keep the hoppers full of food and the trays clean, an idea which must surely recommend itself to the man of the house!

It's well known that an unhappy hen won't lay, and our daily average is very high. We have on many occasions collected 12 eggs in the one day. One can't ask more of a poor hen than that, except to expect her to hop into the oven and cook herself.

I admit my conscience pricks me often when I look at them, but, as it appears to worry me more than it does the hen, I would suggest to all disbelievers that they face facts and stop trying to imagine what it's like to sit in a cage all day.

**Comment.** Like it or not, batteries are here to stay. There **is** a choice for consumers who can now buy free-range eggs, at a higher price. There **are** fairly regular visits into poultry sheds by animal-welfare activists, who are so incensed that they break the law to get ugly photos of the cramped chooks. That, **however**, seems to be the status quo, and I expect it to remain quite status until a hen gets elected into the Senate on a "free the chooks" ticket. Even then, there are many vested interests who will not rollover easily.

## NEWS AND VIEWS

The US Atomic Energy Commission said that it plans today to fire a rocket with **an atomic warhead**. It will climb to a height of **six miles** and, when it explodes, will destroy any planes within a half-mile radius. The world continues to find **new playful ways of exploiting the potential of atomic energy**.

**Airlines in Australia** will create a new class of passenger service **called tourist class. Previously the airlines had only one class, First Class**, but now they will introduce the new seats at a lower price.

## APRIL NEWS ITEMS

**Winston Churchill** is expected to announce his **retirement from politics** tonight, after he has a special dinner with the Queen and Duke. He is currently Prime Minister. **Anthony Eden is tipped as his successor**.

Speed limits for motor cars in all States are **fixed at 30 miles per hour. Outside built up areas, they are generally unlimited.** There are moves afoot **to set a speed limit, of perhaps 50 mph, outside these areas**. The NRMA supports this, and many motorists and other motoring groups oppose it. A poll of motorists was undecided, and ended up about 50 - 50.

April 8th headline: *NEW VIC EXECUTIVE EXPEL 104 BRANCH MEMBERS.* This is typical of the way that the Labor Party is getting into the news. There is no point in trying to work out what is going on. All you need to note is that **the Party is in complete turmoil right round the nation**….

One reason is that the **influence of the Communists within is being challenged by groups organised by the Catholic Church**. Dr Evatt, as leader, is under constant pressure, and is just scraping through from one crisis to the next.

A seven-year-old boy was killed and 20 other spectators were injured by a runaway car at Mt Panorama car racing circuit today. A tyre blew out on an Alfa-Alvis, it careered off the track, then somersaulted onto its front and landed among spectators. This was during the annual races at Bathurst.

The US has declared that **the Salk vaccine**, used in the fight against polio, is 85 per cent effective, and is safe to use. It is expected that with a few months it **will become 100 per cent effective, and could bring complete triumph over polio**....

The Head of the Institute of Epidemiology at Sydney's Prince Henry Hospital said that the serum was **produced from monkey kidneys**. "If we produce it in Australia, sooner or later we are going to encounter **the difficulty of obtaining sufficient monkeys from India** to keep producing the serum."

**The NSW Labor Party is having more problems.** A group of members, already in Parliament, have formed a new party that will be called **Anti-Communist** Labor Party. Clearly, it will split the Labor vote on some matters.

The Federal Government announced that **Australia would definitely have television by the start of the Olympic Games next year**. It said that we would get **four channels by then,** two in Sydney and two in Melbourne.

**April 20ᵗʰ.** Labor Party tension came to the fore in Parliament in a spectacular manner when **seven defectors** from the Parliamentary Party turned their attack on Evatt...

Speakers for the **newly-formed Anti-Communist Labor Party** said that Evatt was the man who wrecked the Labor Party, that he was the best friend that the Communists ever had, and that he had accepted large sums of money from Communist sources. The parade of speakers went on for two hours. Like I said earlier, **the Labor Party is in turmoil**.

The NSW State Government (and other State governments) is about to produce legislation that will ensure that **the buyer on Hire Purchase will pay at least a ten per cent deposit.** This is to protect some buyers from themselves, so that there **is less chance of them defaulting on their deb**t. The interest rate will remain **unregulated** for now (but will be regulated in a few years). At the moment, **the interest rate on HP starts at 12 and goes up to 40 per cent per annum**.

At the moment, in several States, including NSW and Victoria, the **railways systems are protected**. That is, **long-distance interstate hauliers are basically prevented by law from competing with the railways covering the same routes**. Currently, there is agitation to remove these laws, but it seems that the State governments want to keep the profits they earn from rail, **and will be slow to change laws**.

**The new opening hours for pubs** in NSW were causing a few concerns. At a recent referendum, the voters decided that **pubs would shut at 6.30 pm, for an hour. After that, they would re-open till 10pm.** Some pubs, for example in **day-time** factory areas, were saying that they would not re-open because all the workers had gone home by 7.30. **Could, or would, or should, the Government force them to re-open?**

## FOOD IN PACKETS

In 1955, if you wanted Rice Bubbles, you could buy **a packet** of them, and have the pleasure of their snapping, crackling, and popping all through your breakfast. Likewise if you wanted baked beans, or syrup, or condensed milk, you could buy them already packaged.

Packaging was making big inroads into marketing. Raw milk was giving way to bottled. Other foodstuffs were currently changing over. For example, with flour and rolled oats, the shop-keeper no longer went to a big bin and, using a dipper to dig out your serving, put it into a brown paper bag. Now you could buy a packet of Mothers Choice Flour and you would have not only the flour, but would also **be conscious of the brand name**. There was even talk that bread would come wrapped in paper, while on the other hand, meat might soon not be wrapped in newspaper, but in white unused paper.

This change-over reportedly always had advantages. For example, with flour and rolled oats, the packaging system ruled out any chance of weevils, so the advertising said. As it turned out, this was not true. But that will not surprise anyone. Readers of the *SMH* had their different views on what was happening.

**Letters, SH.** Why can housewives seldom buy plain flour in bulk nowadays?

I find that a 2-pound cardboard packet of flour retails for 1/5. While another well-known brand sells for 1/- in a brown paper bag. Thus I am charged 5d for a useless piece of cardboard.

**Letters, HOUSEWIFE.** Flour is only one of many household items now put into packets at much higher prices. To name just a few, gelatine, citric and tartaric acid, carb soda, coconut and raisins.

Things are quite expensive enough without having to pay so much more for the sake of a useless packet.

**Letters, Douglas D Taylor.** How irritating it is to read letters from correspondents which pinpoint fidgety aspects of our economic set-up, but ignore the great essentials.

Someone complains that two pounds of plain flour in a cardboard carton, carrying the imprimatur of a well-known trade name, sells at 1/5, while the same quantity of unbranded flour in a brown paper bag costs only 1/.

Prepackaging at factory level has been one of the greatest factors in reducing the cost of distribution of food. The grocer who used to buy tea by the chest, flour by the bag, kerosene by the drum and other lines in bulk, was obliged to charge a profit of about 35 p.c. on cost.

Today, the food store which handles prepackaged good operates on a profit of about 23 p.c. on cost. Some self-service stores are able to distribute food to the public, making a surcharge of only 15 p.c. on the cost of what they sell.

Then, there is the matter of hygiene. Who wants to eat food that has been mauled by miscellaneous hands, tossed around from bulk bin to paper bag with insanitary scoops and finally served over the counter anonymously?

**Letters, E M B.** "Housewife", by suggesting that the "useless" packet in which gelatine is marketed is an unnecessary expense, shows she has little knowledge of this valuable and useful product and complete ignorance of the Pure Food Act, which is designed to look after her interests.

Under Regulation 21 of the Pure Food Act, 1908-1944, it is laid down that gelatine for human consumption must be of a certain strength and quality, and every package must carry the words "For Food."

The consumer is, therefore, assured of receiving an edible product of high purity and with satisfactory setting properties. No right thinking citizen would wish to see this Act, which so excellently safeguards the health of the community, relaxed.

Although it has been in force for many years, the Act is still flouted deliberately, or though lack of knowledge of the regulations, by some unscrupulous grocers to cater for the penny-wise-pound-foolish housewife.

**Letters, B J F.** It may be true that packaging has saved distribution and handling costs; but, that being the case, it merely emphasises that there is small reason for many packaged foods being so much more expensive than the same foods sold in bulk.

No one has denied that some foods are better packaged; the point of complaint is that the extra charge is excessive – if it is justified at all.

I have in mind the experience, many years ago, of a relative who managed a company producing a fine grade of oatmeal.  This product, put up in 5lb calico bags, did not sell particularly well until an advertising man persuaded the firm to put the meal in 1lb packets and increase the price. After that the product never looked back.

In that case – and I dare say in many – the consumers are the mugs. They show willingness to pay more for less in neat containers, and manufacturers simply take advantage of that.  But when it means that bulk supplies are denied those who are thrifty enough to seek them, complaint becomes timely.

For example, what has become of cheap, pure lime juice such as was available in bulk, unsweetened, at one time? Nowadays one has to pay about 4/ a bottle for the comparatively uneconomical cordial.

**Comment.** In 2016, looking back, it is obvious that packaging and branding have become a huge industry. If you look at a supermarket, and look at the variety of flour on the shelves, you might also notice that there is no way of buying unpackaged in a brown paper bag. This is an industry that, along with advertising and the like, has changed the world we live in.

## OUR TROOPS FOR MALAYA

For months now, Australia had been toying with sending troops to Malaya. We were aware that the country was suffering from an insurgency that stemmed from **two sources**. **One** was the desire of most of the population to be rid of British colonial status, and to establish a nationalist government. **The second source** was driven by Chinese-led Communism that wanted their own forces to establish a Communist state that was, of course, free of the colonialism that most nationals detested.

These two militant bodies had some ideals in common, and they were somehow trying to work towards the common goal of getting rid of the Brits. So they were forming guerrilla groups and small armies that were attacking British settlers, and sometimes openly engaging in small battles with the British Army.

Australia announced on April 1st that we were sending quite large forces to the region. Until now we had sent some advisors, a few non-combat planes, and supplies. Now it was decided that we would send a full battalion of troops, and accompanying naval and Air Force support. It was a considerable commitment.

The Prime Minister, Bob Menzies, argued that we needed to stop the Communist menace that was growing to our North. The Domino Theory said that the nations of South East Asia would **fall** to the Communist hordes one by one, **like dominoes**, and that eventually the Reds would get hold of Tasmania, their ultimate goal. "We must fight our battle against Communism as far North of Australia as possible."

The Leader of our Opposition, Doc Evatt, thought Menzies was wrong. He wanted Australia to actively seek better relationships with Asia, and he knew that China would react badly to the troops.

**Comment**. Menzies had a long-standing habit of talking about *Reds under the Beds* whenever he wanted a few votes. He was a Red-baiter from way back, and had never hesitated to play the Red card when it suited him. Still, there can be no doubt that he did see the international Reds as a genuine long-term menace, and his decision to send troops stemmed from this, with the happy side-effect that it boosted his credentials at home.

Evatt's policy was quite different. Basically he said that, in Cambodia, Vietnam, Laos, and Malaya, **the nationals should be given self-rule as fast as possible**, and if that were granted, the appeal of Communism would go away. It was only **because the moves towards nationalism were being frustrated** that the Reds could gather support.

There were plenty of Letter-writers with opinions. Mr Quek, a Malayan student of Croydon Park, was shocked that Dr Evatt opposed the sending of troops. "Clearly, he does not understand the national movement of the Malayan people," and he urged him to go there for a fact-finding visit.

In a second Letter, he was not so wishy-washy.

**Letters, Seng Hin Quek, NSW University of Technology.** About 60 per cent of the people of Malaya are Malays (the true native of Malaya). They also constitute nearly all the Malayan armed forces which are fighting the terrorists.

The terrorists in Malaya are not Malayan citizens; they are aliens in our country. I, being a Malayan, can safely say that the purpose of the Australian Government in sending troops to Malaya will be gladly supported.

There are Malayans who are afraid to help the Malayan Government wipe out the terrorists because they are not sure that the British Government and other democratic countries will always protect Malaya from being taken by the Communists.

I am sure that the arrival of Australian forces in Malaya will considerably increase the morale of the Malayans in their fight against the terrorists.

His is not the only opinion.

**Letters, D Hobson (Vicar of Penang, 1950-51).** If our policies cause a reaction which we do not anticipate, then they will do damage to our relations with South-East Asia which we do not desire. It is the strong possibility of this that disturbs me in recent decisions by our Government which until recently has had a good record of much constructive work in Australian-Asian relations.

Mr Menzies has said that the Government's decision to send troops to Malaya will make clear to Asian people that we intend to stop the march of Communism in South-East Asia. But the effect may be that it **will assist the spread of Communism in South-East Asia** because it will be interpreted by many thoughtful Asians **as a new imperialism intended to block self-government in Malaya.**

Feeling on this question of self-government is running high in Malaya. Mr Menzies's statement that our battles for our defence will have to be **fought far from Australia's shores** may sound common sense to us, but **it will sound like imperialism to many people in Asia** and will no doubt be exploited to the full by Communist propaganda.

The real danger is that our resort to force may seem to Asians to cover for **spiritual degeneracy in us** and for Asians, spiritual and moral values are important.

**Comment.** Who was right? There were very different views, on a matter that would cost Australian lives. What would you have thought at the time? What do you think now in the light of history?

## TWO VIEWS OF DESECRATION

**Letters, Jessie Boyd.** A **sugar** model of the Cenotaph exhibited at the Royal Show was awarded third prize – as a cake decoration.

That the entry should have been accepted as an exhibit was disgraceful. In awarding a prize, the judges virtually set the seal of the society's approval on an act, however unthinking, which amounts to **desecration** by belittlement of a symbol sacred to all Australians.

**Letters, Pierre Haugh.** About fourteen years ago, I witnessed German troops punishing a village in Austria. They attacked the small cathedral with mortars and grenades, destroyed the altar and all the statues and paintings, stole anything of value, piled the pews and furniture into a heap and set fire to them inside the cathedral, then took two priests and shot them in the town square.

**That**, Jessie Boyd, was desecration.

## FOOD AND DRINK

**I am a hamburger eater**. Over the years, I have eaten all sorts of food, in many different restaurants and dives. Some of it has been too sophisticated for words, and some of it the almost-barbarous dingo stew. So, you might expect that when I say the good old-fashioned hamburger is about my favourite food, I am not speaking from complete ignorance.

Of course, it has to be the **old-fashioned** hamburger. **It cannot be a fast-food burger.** It cannot be a plastic bun, with its hunk of still-frozen meat paste, dill pickle, and a scrape of mayonnaise, pushed out in under a minute. With shredded lettuce, would you believe. Let me elaborate.

My ideal hamburger, a la 1955, has to be made in a small shop, probably a milk-bar, run by an Italian or Greek family, with the mum and children often sitting on stools out of the way. The dad has to be sweaty, standing over a hotplate, taking orders over his shoulder, while a son or daughter chops the beetroot, tomato, and onion, and wraps up the end product. The meat has to be proper minced meat, with real blood dribbling off the wooden cutting-board. The beetroot is essential, and it has to be so fresh that its juice will dribble down onto your shirt at the first bite. No hamburger is complete without burnt onion rings.

Other essentials include a wait of at least 15 minutes, so that you have the time to drink a small Coca Cola, in its classic shaped bottle. The burger must be eventually wrapped in newspaper, and it must be eaten quickly so that the grease will not soften it till the burger sticks to the paper. A juke box is important, with "Rock Around the Clock" played at least once each visit.

Alas, though, it is getting difficult to find anywhere that sells such delicacies. In the City of Newcastle, 50 years ago a mecca for good burgers, I can count current vendors on the fingers of one hand. It seems that the need for speed, and the not unnatural desire for cleanliness, has allowed US chains to out-sell the local Italian and Greek boys.

Well, so much for good food. **What about good drinks?** Here I am not talking about alcohol, or fizzy sweet stuff. Rather I mean beverages, hot beverages, the drinks that everyone sips throughout the day, and without which the world would stop spinning.

**In 1955, I can only be talking about tea.** Not instant tea, in a little satchel, that you steeped directly in your cup. That came later. No, I mean real tea, the tea that you bought in a quarter-pound packet at the grocers. Tea that came from companies that had already realised the value of branding, so that you had the choice of Bushells, in a blue-packet, or Kinkara, in a green packet. A little later, Billy was added to the list, in a white and orange packet, if I remember correctly.

Once you had the packet, the burning question that kept turning up was, **how do you prepare a good cuppa?** I will allow Letter-writers to take over. The first Letter started the ball rolling.

**Letters, K A H Read, Commissioner, The Tea Bureau, Sydney.** In the June, 1954, edition of the Journal of the American Medical Association, two notable conclusions are recorded in an article. One is that tea tones up the stomach muscles, which tend to get "tired" when overloaded with a large meal. Any heavy meal, especially one containing much food, leaves the stomach sooner when followed by a cup of tea. The second conclusion is that tea makes the stomach no more acid than does a cup of hot water, so it cannot be harmful even to people with duodenal or stomach ulcers.

**Letters, R Kellett.** The letter from the Tea Bureau Commissioner omits mention that tea is often overbrewed.

It has become well known to those whose business it is to watch over the public health that the popular and refreshing beverage under discussion is not healthy if the brewing is prolonged over five minutes. Indeed, in England, health authorities recommend only four and a half minutes.

These facts should be more widely known than is the case; tea should be off the leaves under five minutes.

**Letters, E D.** Brewing tea for five minutes may be quite right in theory, but is no good in practice for people who like strong tea as we do.

Even when the tea is brewed for a longer time one is likely to get a strong first and a weak second cup.

As the Commonwealth pays a large subsidy on tea, and as we still pay a high price in spite of the subsidy, it is time the "powers that be" roused themselves and saw to it that they, and we, got value for money (or is 1st-grade tea merely a myth?).

**Letters, W Hoy.** When brewing tea, the entire ritual is conducted to suit the palate of the drinker.

However, in normal cases it is first useful to know that tea is composed of four main parts: Flavouring oils, caffeine, natural colouring matter, and a substance similar to tannin.

After freshly boiling water has been added to the dry leaf, the quickly-melting flavouring oils and caffeine, plus most of the colouring matters, have passed to the brew at the end of five minutes.

The liquor should be strained off into a second heated teapot, and is then ready for serving.

**Letters, C M.** I am a chronic tea-drinker and I think it runs in the family. My father has been accused of bathing in tea, so much of it does he consume.

Very conservatively, I figure that we have consumed a total of 260,000 cups of tea so far in our lifetime.

We were both rather shaken to read that some of your correspondents ill-treat the beverage to the extent of stewing it for five and even 10 minutes.

There is only one way to drink tea – while it is hot, and before it changes from a delicacy to a powerful tanning agent.

We have both found that one minute is the ideal brewing time. Ten minutes' tea brewing should be included in the capital offences.

**Comment.** Now that you are much the wiser, I would like to have a quick look at how the beverage world has changed in the last 60 years. Obviously, in Australia the rise and rise of coffee has changed things a lot. Over the years, instant coffee, with its 43 beans in every cup, made big sales. More recently have come the new founded coffee shops, and these have blossomed into US chains like Gloria Jeans and

Starbucks. As well, every office worker today has access to a coffee machine, or goes out twice a day to get a plastic cup of the life-giving stimulant.

**Silently, though, tea has made a comeback.** There are dozens, perhaps hundreds, of varieties of teas on the shelves, and people everywhere are gradually getting their own fine-china cups, that supposedly make the tea taste the way they like it. Tea has developed a growing cult of its own, and while it looked to be on its last legs 20 years ago, it is clearly on the comeback trail. We should all keep an eye on it over the next 60 years.

# YOUR HANDY GUIDE TO PIG SHOOTING

**Letters, K E P, Tumut.** In my opinion, Mr W O Bluett's article about wild pigs on the Monaro contains several rather misleading statements.

As a huntsman of wild pigs for many years I have never been in danger. If savagely bailed up by dogs, pigs defend themselves but will escape to thick scrub at the first opportunity. I have caught young squealing suckers and the mother sow, on most occasions, beats a hasty retreat.

A bushman captures the pigs with the assistance of dogs and carries them back to camp or farm house, if not too large, or on the pack horse. They are then dressed as a sheep is. The meat baked or boiled fresh is really delicious. Dairyfarmers grow and fatten such pigs or breed from them. Like the brumby, they soon become quiet and do particularly well, and are free from disease.

Myxomatosis has not spread to many large areas of the great National Park. Lack of mosquitoes in the higher cooler regions could be the reason. A very contagious mange, which has spread rapidly among foxes, causing their deaths in great numbers over a period of years, has enabled young pigs to exist and breed.

**Letters, W J Owens.** First, the .22 calibre rifle definitely is not of sufficient power for pig or kangaroo shooting. I have killed pigs with it up to 100 yards and more, but it is too "chancy" and a hit must be dead centre.

Secondly, the shoulder shot is not effective against an old boar. Frequent fights have developed, on his shoulders, a protective shield of thick hide which will flatten a leaden bullet. The shot should be aimed behind the shoulder for the heart. The kidney shot below the backbone is deadly, but with a pig on the run it is not on the programme for even a moderately good shot.

For close work, such as walking up to a wounded boar, the shotgun is the best weapon. A quick side-step to avoid a charging pig and a charge of No. 3 behind the ear at a distance of five or six feet spells finis to the toughest pig.

## NEWS AND VIEWS

**The coming of TV will provide new problems** for people to worry about. **Can a sporting event be subject to copyright?** Can one Channel pay a sporting body some money, and then say that they have the right to air an event **exclusively**? If another Channel wants to show some short clips, does it have to pay for them? These were very different problems for the growing TV industry, and it would be fair to say that now, despite being mainly resolved, **they can still cause headaches**....

Remember when the **Test cricket was shown simultaneously** by all three TV networks of the time? And broadcast by three different radio networks?

## MAY NEWS ITEMS

May 2nd. Popular American actress**, Betty Hutton**, flew into Sydney for a 17-day tour. She was well known here for her role in the movie **Annie Get your Gun.** She was, as usual by now, mobbed at the airport….

The next day, **Katherine Hepburn**, the actress partner of Spencer Tracy, flew in for a few months' tour. She will join the **Old Vic Shakespearean** Company and do a six-month season of three plays….

She arrived with **renowned ballet dancer, Australian Robert Helpmann** who, strangely enough, **will act in those same plays**. There was a sedate group of 100 people at the airport to greet the pair….

Helpmann has not been to Australia for 25 years. His acting parts will include Shylock in *The Merchant of Venice.*

May 6th. West Germany had been created during the **partitioning of Germany** proper after WWII. Today it was **granted the status of an independent nation**, and can now make its own laws and defence decisions. Austria was freed from 20-years of foreign occupation a few days later.

**Politics and religion were in the news.** The Catholic Bishops stated that the way to **fight Communism** was for it to do battle within the Trade Unions and the Labor Party. It re-iterated its support for the so-called Groupers who **stood in all elections against the Reds**….

Many Protestant Churches, led by the **Methodists,** thought they could get a better result by **helping people** with economic needs, and those suffering from social injustice. "A responsible society, built on Christian principles, makes any kind of totalitarian society impossible".

The **Federal Government tabled an independent report on our mental institutions** that referred to "hopeless" overcrowding, filthy conditions, "woeful" staff shortages, and an appalling lack of proper treatment and equipment.

News for **Rugby League fans. The French team has arrived** in Australia for a two-month tour. **Watch out for punch-ups.**

In the NSW country city of Bathurst, the Council appealed to **the CSIRO for help in driving away hundreds of starlings from the city's War Memorial**. The CSIRO suggested **holding a starling by its legs, and have its piercing screeches and alarm-calls recorded. Then re-playing it** at amplified levels at the roosts of the starlings....

A Melbourne bird expert said that such methods had been tried overseas without much success. "Starlings are pretty shrewd birds. **They will probably realise that it is a fake**...."

"In Melbourne, they tried to frighten pigeons with a stuffed owl, but after a while the pigeons got used to it, and **perched next to it."**

**Seat bookings opened today for the Olympic Games** in Melbourne next year. Sales were heavy. All the tickets for the **night swimming events have already been sold out**.

**A hundred young Cynomolgus monkeys**, to be used in the production of the Salk vaccine, will be flown into Melbourne today. **Scientists will remove their kidney tissue, from which vaccine will be made.** A single monkey can provide **enough vaccine for about 1,000 doses**....

Batches of monkeys will arrive in Melbourne **every two or three weeks from now on**.

The exciting prospect of **drive-in cinemas** moved closer to reality when it was announced that **14 licences would be granted in NSW**. Twelve of these would be Sydney, while Newcastle and Wollongong would each get one.

In Adelaide race meeting at Morphettville, South Australia, a jockey was disqualified **after a battery was found by the Chief Steward**. He became suspicious when the horse dropped in the betting from 33 to 7-1. The steward visited the jockeys' quarters, and when he picked up the jockey's whip, **received an electric shock**. The jockey was ousted for 10 years. The horse's trainer also got 10 years.

In the **Victorian State elections, the Labor Party appears to have lost 20 seats**. Voters can read the papers.

News item, May 31st. **Australia's Davis Cup squad** left for England. It included Ken Rosewall and Neale Fraser.

The Bathurst Gun Club accepted an invitation from the Council to **shoot the starlings** that were being a nuisance at the city's War Memorial. They thus fired 350 rounds of ammunition at the starlings as they massed at dusk, and **killed 500 of them and 12 pigeons**....

The birds made no attempt to disperse, and instead **tried to get to their perches**. The Park's Curator said that the shoot would be repeated next week if necessary. About 200 persons watched the shootings, and many of them were schoolchildren.

**Australia has a mandate from the UN, to administer New Guinea**. This means that the regulations set for the population **there** are different from the laws in Australia....

**In New Guinea, floggings are still handed out as punishment** for offences by juveniles, sexual offences, violence, and prison offences. **Females are exempted.**

**Pope Pius XII** warned the world against the dangers of **provoking sterility in mankind by the reckless use of radio-active sources**. He spoke of "**the horrors of monstrous offspring**" that might result from the damage to parental genes.

The Minister for Immigration, Harold Holt, welcomed **our one-millionth migrant since the war** in Melbourne. **Comment.** That's a lot of new people for a nation of this size.

# NUCLEAR BOMB DAMAGE

For the last decade, the atom bomb in its many forms has been at the forefront of thoughtful minds. When the bombs were first dropped on Japan, it was claimed that **nuclear energy** could bring many advantages as well as destruction, and much was written on the subject. Over the years, though, it has been the development of **the bomb** that has dominated the media, and which claims our attention at this time.

The bomb that was once a simple atom bomb has now developed into a hydrogen bomb, and would soon enough become a neutron variety. It has been tested in deserts, the atmosphere, under water, underground, and perhaps soon in the stratosphere. Little ones have been developed, nuclear tips would soon appear, rockets can launch them. Many of mankind's best scientific brains were dedicated to finding bigger and better ways to annihilate a potential enemy. This fact alone was provoking people the world over to look again at the consequence of this nuclear arms race that the world was locked into.

So it was timely when a series of Letters arrived, each of them in their own way pointing out the dangers of nuclear war and the folly of the **current** attempts to reduce their damage. Many of these Letters came from the Physics Departments of the nation's Universities and so they carried with them the authority that scientists in those days enjoyed. John Blatt, from the Physics Department of Sydney University, was particularly forceful.

He, and others, pointed out that it was silly to say that Sydney could not be attacked. It only took a couple of planes to A-bomb the cities in Japan, and these were protected by a war-time defence force. Sydney in peace time would be a sitting duck.

Further, even if there was a warning that we had a few hours' notice that an attack was imminent, there was no way that a city of millions of people could evacuate in the time available. Think of the chaos that would prevail.

The scientists went on to say that a large hydrogen bomb would kill almost everyone within a ten-mile radius. That would include all of Sydney at the time. No one would survive. It was hopeless to say that shelters could be built for millions of people, or that these people could get to them in time. There would be no living persons left.

On top of this the radioactivity, as a war progressed, would grow to the stage that the entire world would be threatened. There is no way to avoid this or to reduce this. Once it arrives, it is here to stay, it permeates everywhere, and even underground living for decades will be impossible.

Suppose somehow there were survivors. Every reproductive adult would have their genes damaged so that the most horrible birth mutations would happen, and the world would descend into a place peopled by the most grotesqe characters. Most likely, the next generations would not be able to reproduce, and that was another path to extinction.

Suppose too that people on the fringe areas of the bomb could be saved by shelters and other civil defence measures. That would not help, because they too would receive an impossibly high dose of radiation, and while they might live, they too would be genetically damaged and probably physically as well. They would have bad seed, and damage the human race.

The scientists were emphatic that talking about civil defence matters was giving a false sense of security. People felt that something was being done, that the authorities had the matter in hand, and that there was after all almost an assurance that they would survive.

The scientists, en masse, and in their own way, ended by agreeing with Blatt's contention that **civil defence would not only fail to save the vast majority of Australian city dwellers from a horrible death; it would be worse than useless against the main threat, which is the very likely complete annihilation of the whole human race by the delayed, genetic effects.**

The *SMH* was keen to get into the fray. In fact, so eager was it that it published its **editorial s**emi-rebuttal on the **same day** as it published Blatt's Letter. First of all**, it agreed** that "there is no defence against an atomic attack on Sydney. **Nearly all those within a 10-mile radius would be killed.**"

It then brought out the inevitable **but's. But**, it said, Sydney would probably have a few days or a week's notice, and in that period, an evacuation for **women and children** could be managed. **Bu**t, it said, the radio-active peril "is theoretically possible, but it is not certain". It added nothing else on this matter. **But,** it said, that we should see it as **our Christian duty** to send aid to survivors, despite the **danger** of radiation damage. Blatt would have said "despite the **certainty** of **radiation** damage. **Why make the problem bigger?**"

There were other Letters. A few suggested that a planned and **deliberate dispersal** of the population over many years would mitigate against a bomb's effects. Another pointed out that the atomic cloud would **probably drift out to sea**, and that **might** reduce the radiation damage.

One evacuation advocate suggested an unusual part-solution.

> **Letters, Wentworth Huyshe. Evacuation** is the only feasible solution of the problem. It calls for meticulous planning and organising.
>
> One great task would be to organise the receiving centres for the evacuees.
>
> I would suggest the seeking of the cooperation of the thousands of graziers throughout the country, to make available the **accommodation in their shearing sheds**. Accommodation varies, according to the size of the property, and would range, roughly, between 20 and 80 men, with an average of, say, 30 men.
>
> This number takes into consideration the standard accommodation only, and could be practically doubled, in an emergency, by using work-rooms for men and boy evacuees. The standard facilities conform to regulations – they are permanent, well-equipped, and could be made available at very short notice.
>
> Between 1939 and 1942, I was in civil defence in London. I know that if some definite and workable plan is not drawn up – and the people drilled to do their part – chaos will reign.

Another raised a legitimate concern about how the authorities **were asking for trouble** by concentrating activities in the most likely target area.

**Letters, A H Goodwin.** Apparently, Government authorities do not realise that they are arranging an ideal target for any future hostile force.

We have a situation where the whole State could practically be crippled in one blow.

Not only is this city vulnerable from the air, but we are also making this target within range from the sea.

A Civic Defence Council is about to set up. Decentralisation and dispersal is its main ally, but if the method of concentrating all vital services is continued, then its job, so far as Sydney is concerned, will become neutralised and well nigh impossible.

Let us have some practical military thought on the matter before we make it too easy for any future enemy.

A number of writers said again that **a Christian society is bound to give aid** to survivors at all costs. Several were concerned, not with the provision of aid to survivors, but with **the survival of the entire human race**. Several Letter-writers called for **the Great Powers to renounce for all times their sovereign rights to manufacture and use nuclear weapons of all kinds**.

The Blatt Letter generated a lot of heat and some light. I will close this discussion with the final paragraph from a second Letter that Blatt sent. He re-stated his position: Once the radioactivity has been let loose, there is no effective way of stopping it. This is a major issue at present, and talk about "military superiority", "civil defence", and blind "Christian faith in our survival" merely beclouds the issue.

**Comment.** At the time the Blatt Letter was published, I was finishing a degree at Sydney University. I was 21 years of age, and not at all concerned with matters of survival of the human race. Most of the time, **I knew** that, whatever happened, **I** would survive OK. I would live forever, if not longer. It was **other people** who got sick and died.

In the few moments that I thought about things serious, I reasoned that nobody would be so stupid as to unleash a bomb. Everyone knew that retaliation would be immediate, and that civilisation would be destroyed. So, in my own philistine way, I developed the theory of **mutual** destruction that keeps the world as safe as it is today.

## HIRE PURCHASE FOR THE NAÏVE

Hire Purchase was the next big thing. It was sweeping the land, and it made easy the borrowing of money to purchase household items and gadgets. If you were riding the economic boom, and you had a good income, and were paying off a new house, then why wait till you had saved the money before you took possession of the goods that you wanted? You could borrow the money, and take the lot home right now. It was so simple.

You could get a car, a fridge, a lawn mower, a sofa, a radio, some new form of ghetto-blaster, and bikes for the ankle-biters all at once. Just a reasonable deposit, and then 60 easy monthly payments. It did not matter that you already had a whacking great mortgage hanging over your head. These giant new HP companies would scarcely be worried by a small matter like that.

So, the households of the nation quickly went into deeper debt. There was nothing wrong with this. It was a bit of a gamble, but times were good and the future looked prosperous for most. The trouble was that HP was not as benign as most people thought at the time. As it turned out,

**the interest charged was at double the rate that a bank would charge.**

Borrowers were now starting to get into financial trouble. More trouble than before HP was available. So, legislators were getting anxious about the dangers and lack of regulation of the HP industry, and were starting to make noises about its traps for the unwary.

**Letters, Leslie Haylen.** No sensible person objects to time payment. The judicious use of terms is a great factor in maximum production and full employment. But when the worker's margin disappears in high interest rates for his car, his refrigerator, and his labour-saving gadgets bought on terms at excessive interest rates, and the Serviceman looks glumly at the waiting list of 17,000 for war service homes alone, it is obvious that something is wrong.

The home-hungry feel aggrieved when the banks refuse them any assistance on long-term building loans, but rush the short-term requirements of the cash order and finance firms.

There is a job for the States here to **re-examine the interest rate** in time-payment agreements for the benefit of the worker and the economy.

# REACTIONS TO SALK

The public reaction to the Salk vaccine was immediate. Almost everyone wanted it **now**, though there were a few dragging their feet.

**Letters, F B.** I am utterly disgusted with the reaction of Australian medical authorities (Commonwealth and State) to the new American Salk polio vaccine.

The Federal Minister for Health declared that "it was not quite clear how effective the vaccine was." The

Commonwealth Director of Health said that "if the new vaccine measured up to its claims, it would be a year before production could begin in Australia." The NSW Minister for Health declared that "immunisation would be considered when the efficacy was proved, and sufficient supplies were available."

One Sydney doctor remarked that millions of monkeys would be required for general immunisation. Apart from America, where there is known to be everything, it appears that there are millions of monkeys also in Denmark, because this country will immunise all children free of charge.

**Letters, Oscar Guth.**  Parents all over the world, were they to read Mrs O Mackey's statement in the "Herald" of April 22, would be shocked to think that a woman could voice such sentiments.

Mrs Mackey, honorary secretary of the Australian branch of the World League for the Protection of Animals, **advocates an Indian export ban on monkeys vital for the production of the Salk anti-polio vaccine.**

She says her organisation does not think it justified to take the life of an animal to save that of a human being.

Surely, every mother in the world, would gladly sacrifice all the monkeys in existence to save her child.  Would Mrs Mackey's organisation rather preserve monkeys and let humans continue to die of polio?

**Comment.**  In fact, Australia was as quick off the mark as anyone else was. The numbers of polio cases dropped away very quickly, and when the Sabin vaccine was added to the medical arsenal in a few years, the incidence dropped to almost zero.

## JUNE NEWS ITEMS

**American comedian, Bob Hope, was mobbed last night** by 1,700 people at Sydney's Theatre Royal when he attended the **world premiere of his new movie,** *The Seven Little Foys.* He got the normal hero's welcome, with ladies fainting, confetti, guests in tuxedos and elegant dresses. He addressed the audience for 15 minutes, and **took it all with good grace.**

The NSW Chief Secretary recently conducted a survey of the accommodation provided by **Sydney's hotels.** He found that 360 of them provided only **drinking facilities, and no beds at all.** Very few of the other hotels provided reasonable bedding....

He concluded that Sydney's hotel accommodation was poor compared to Melbourne's, and that overseas tourists were badly catered for. He mentioned that the **situation in the country was even worse. Amen to all of that.**

The **mice plague** in Warwick, a largish Queensland town, has become so bad that "**cats have gone on strike**", and take no notice of the mice.

Police in Sydney are about to enforce a Regulation that allows them to **tow away illegally parked vehicles.** The offending motorist must pay **a fine and towing expenses.**

The Queen's Birthday Honours list **included a knighthood for Eugene Goossens**, the conductor of the Sydney Symphony Orchestra.

A man was run over **and killed while sleeping on a railway line at Nyngan** in NSW country. He was lying on a rarely-used track, when a shunting train cut off his legs.

The four Eastern States of Australia have been **taxing trucks that carried freight across State boundaries**. Now, the Full High Court has found that such actions interfere with free trade, **and that their taxes are illegal**. It also ordered the States to repay taxes already paid. **This was a big win for road hauliers.**

**85 people were killed and 120 were injured when a racing car plunged off the track** at a 24-hour road-race at **Le Mans raceway in France**. A German Mercedes somersaulted over the rails and into the crowded embankment. The Mercedes exploded, and the engine, wheels, and other parts catapulted shoulder-high into the tightly-packed mass of spectators.

The Commonwealth Government will abandon **its controls over tea (imposed during the war)**, and the price of tea is expected to fall by about 8 per cent.

There are 158 entries so far in this year's **Redex round-Australia car trial**.

**Polio has killed a young scientist engaged in polio research at Adelaide.** He caught the disease while working with polio virus cultures at the Institute of Medical and Veterinary Research.

**The Olympic Games continues to sell well.** 325,000 reserved seats, out of 1,250,000, have been sold.

# KILLING OF BIRDS AT BATHURST

Those birds at Bathurst were killed right at the end of May, , so that Letters about the one-sided shoot-out came through in June. The first respondents were decidedly against the fuselage.

**Letters, (Miss) Margaret E Seibert.** I wish to place on record my protest at the unreasonable destruction of birds in the Bathurst War Memorial Carillon Tower.

This slaughter of innocent bird-life, witnessed by a large number of children of impressionable age, violated the basic rules of kindness and love for all helpless creatures.

While appreciating the necessity for something to be done, I cannot believe that the worthy gentlemen of the Bathurst City Council are without feeling in this matter, and therefore I cannot understand why a screen, as suggested, was not tried first before the other drastic step was taken.  If it were a matter of expense beyond the council's budget, I'm sure an appeal to bird-lovers in this State would have brought strong support.

The cost of ammunition would have gone a long way towards the other and more humane method of attempting to deal with the problem.

**Letters, A Citizen of Bathurst.** I hope your readers will not think that the slaughter of hundreds of starlings at Bathurst reflects the true feeling of all the town's citizens towards these birds.

The trouble caused by the starling infestation of the War Memorial tower must be trifling compared to the merry life and picturesque charm which the birds bring to the aerial loneliness of this stark brick column.

After that came an interesting Letter that the *SMH* published under the heading on "Starlings Accused."

**Letters, S W.**  The reference of "A Citizen of Bathurst" to "…. the merry life and picturesque charms" which starlings bring amused me.

Three months ago my family and I developed what we diagnosed as hives.  A friend asked if any starlings were about the house, and suggested that I should inspect the beds.

I found the woodwork and bedding alive with almost colourless mites.  I sprayed the beds and burnt fume sticks.  Every morning for two weeks my family and I had to get under a hot shower as soon as we left our beds.

These mites breed on humans, and we suffered misery.

I am told that when starlings leave the nests, the remaining mites come into the house through windows and ventilators looking for new hosts.

My family and I simply refuse to be gracious hosts next season – an exterminating firm will be asked to do all it can to destroy "the birds' merry life and picturesque charms."

Another supporter of the shooting had his say.

**Letters, L C Haines.**  The recent slaughter of starlings at Bathurst seems to have caused a wild outburst of protest from various bird-lovers.

It is interesting to observe that the starling, apart from being an introduced species and a pest, is also an outrageous menace towards some of our own native birds, particularly those which select hollow trees for nesting purposes.

To mention a few, the tree-creepers, smaller kinds of parrots and some kingfishers.

I have witnessed on numerous occasions the brown tree-creeper and red-backed parrot harassed by starlings until they are forced to depart, and the pugnacious starlings take over the nesting-site and raise their brood.

The only damage the shooting could possibly do is to induce some boys to do likewise to our own useful species.

It is regrettable, indeed, that the same outburst of public sympathy is completely lacking when fine pieces of woodland and swamp, the homes of many beautiful and useful birds, are destroyed or drained, in most cases for no useful purpose at all, the result being complete annihilation of the feathered inhabitants.

Finally, with a more philosophical bent, this writer pointed out that the problem was one that was by no means unique to Bathurst.

**Letters, J W Evans, The Australian Museum, Sydney.** The City Fathers of Bathurst, smarting under the opprobrium of bird-lovers, may find comfort in the thought that if, in fact, they have deterred starlings permanently from roosting on the War Memorial Tower, they will have gained the envy of their opposite numbers in other towns.

Once of the most spectacular sights of London is the arrival in Trafalgar Square at dusk of hundreds of thousands of starlings, intent on spending the night on the surrounding buildings.

Committees at the very highest level have met in Whitehall to plan the destruction of these persistent birds.

When, after long deliberation, traps were chosen as the most promising method of control and some were placed on top of the National Gallery, the result was that two birds were caught in as many weeks.

Likewise in Washington, where stuffed owls, silent noise, gramophone records of distressed starlings, electric shocks, sticky bands and every other method short of shooting has been tried, the starlings are said to have shown their appreciation of these efforts by showering applause on the participants – and still remain.

## GAOL SENTENCES BY PARLIAMENT

The Federal Parliament took the most unusual step of summoning two journalists to appear before it in Canberra today. They were Frank Browne and Raymond Fitzgerald, both employed by the local Bankstown *Observer* newspaper.

This followed a series of articles in which the pair suggested that the local Member was involved in an immigration racket, that he had lost his honour, and was unfit to be a Member. Mr Fitzgerald also admitted that one purpose of the articles was to intimidate the member (Mr Morgan) to vote favourably on issues in Parliament.

The Parliamentary Privileges Committee considered that this was a breach of Privilege, and that the Two Houses of Parliament should question the two men. They did this on the morning of 10th of June. They decided, by a large margin, that the pair was guilty of breaches, and that they should each be sentenced to three month's gaol.

This action by the House raised issues never before discussed in Australia. Everyone was familiar with people being arraigned before the Courts, and sentenced to a period in gaol. Here, however, **it was Parliament itself doing the sentencing**, and doing so in a manner not consistent with the normal rules and procedures.

**For example**, the accused were not allowed to use lawyers to speak for them, they were given no chance of cross-examination, they had no time to prepare a defence. They were tried and sentenced within a few hours, at the end of a session that was about to conclude. Surely, this was undue haste and certainly not due process.

**Letters and protests poured in.** Some of them doubted that the whole process was legal. It had never been used in Australia since Federation, and now, 50 years after that event, it was pulled out of the hat in a most dubious way. **Had the relevant Statutes passed over to Australia in the making of the Constitution?**

Opponents and proponents were vocal and vociferous. I include a small sample of their writings.

The Editor of the *SMH* fired the first bullets. He wrote that the problem arose because, when Australia became independent in 1901, it had not been decided whether or not we should follow the British in allowing for Parliament to try and censure offenders against breaches of privilege in Parliament.

So that this nation had been going along for 54 years, blithely unconcerned that such a situation would arise. But now the question was being asked: did Parliament have the authority to impose gaol terms on violators?

The Government in power had decided that it did, and this got the Editor riled. He said that they did not have the authority until such time as the Parliament debated the issue, and decided on what powers it had.

The Editor pointed out, that in this case, the offenders had no idea of what penalty they might face, and indeed the Parliament itself had no such idea. He, and others, talked about the denial of natural justice, and that the defendants had no right to legal counsel, and that they did not have the right to cross examine, they had no time to prepare a defence, and no arguments from precedent that they could bring forward.

In effect, it was a decision by a group of Parliamentarians, each of them anxious to get home at the end of the Session, who had no knowledge of the laws at issue, and who operated outside the constraints that normally applied in such matters.

The Editor went on to say that it was true that the debate on the issue was in fact conducted with dignity and fairness, except for the contribution of Dr Evatt. But he ended with the opinion that the sentence passed was severe in the extreme. He argued that the House should have had access to the whole evidence and not just selected parts of it before it made up its mind.

So that, and here he was supported by a multitude of writers, the whole matter should have been given greater scrutiny with more deliberation at every stage. All writers agreed that the two defendants deserved to be punished, but the process had been unfair and wanting. Several writers used the terms "kangaroo court" and "bush lawyers".

C E W Bean saw the matter altogether differently. Bean was a distinguished figure who had been given the task, by the Australian Government, of writing the official Australian history of WWI. He had done so, and his many volumes commanded much respect.

He was of the opinion that this nation had the right to be sure that our representatives sent to Parliament should have the unfettered right to complete freedom from any sort of intimidation, both inside and outside the House.

He noted that this right had seldom been attacked in recent years, but he urged that our society should hold grimly to the safeguards we had for the right to free speech by our representatives.

Thus he saw the actions of Parliament, in imposing sentences, as necessary, especially in the light of recent threats of gangsterism, both internal and international. It is pleasing that **this safeguard against a dangerous evil had been so swiftly and moderately used.**

**Letters, Iain McDougall.** The action of Federal Parliament has come as a shock to those who cherish the liberty of the individual and the principle of fair trial in accordance with impartial laws.

The Prime Minister may come to regret the precedent he urged the House to set – to put beyond doubt its right to imprison a citizen without allowing him the benefit of legal representation, or the right of appeal, or the right to question his accusers, or the right to a public trial before a jury of his peers.

The alleged faults of the men imprisoned have no bearing on the propriety of Parliament's action; had they been charged with murder or treason, **they would have been entitled to a fair trial.**

Before this Parliament's precedent becomes firmly established, citizens should ask themselves whether or not they are surrendering the principle of free speech, without which the flower of democracy withers and dies.

Furthermore, on the question of privilege, there are many who think politicians already enjoy privilege to a dangerous and unhealthy degree.

On Friday, Mr Calwell referred to one of the men brought to the Bar of the House in terms that would have provided ample ground for a libel action if uttered elsewhere.

The very word privilege is un-Australian; it smacks of the injustices and social inequalities of older lands.

Finally, it would be well for Australians on this occasion to recall Lord Acton's much-quoted verity: "Power corrupts, absolute power corrupts absolutely."

**Letters, Sydney Counsel.** Mr Morgan had been agitating for a Royal Commission into the state of bribery and corruption allegedly existing in Bankstown; Fitzpatrick, he said, tried to silence him by threatening a denigration campaign, which Fitzpatrick later put into effect. The alleged attempt to silence Morgan was the breach of privilege.

As Morgan himself pointed out in his speech, he could not take Fitzpatrick and Browne to the ordinary Courts – which is what your editorial seems to require – because the matter could then have been sub judice, and Mr Morgan would have been as effectively silenced as if he had yielded to threats.

Mr Morgan, therefore, did not "invoke the ancient and outmoded sanctions of privilege," as you put it, but took the only course open to him, since the ordinary Courts would indirectly protect the wrongdoers.

**Dame Mary Gilmore** was, by now, famous for her writings on social issues, and had long been a prolifiic writer in the newspapers. She had an interesting point to add, and her point of view was supported by other writers.

They said that the **separation of powers** was part of our Constitution. That is, it was the task of the Parliaments to make the law, and it was up to the courts to administer them, and to make punishments for breaches and non-acceptance. **The Parliament had no place in deciding who broke the laws nor in setting punishments.**

Further, Dame Gilmore said, in making laws, Parliaments should occupy itself with enacting progressive laws. They should not spend their time resurrecting old and obsolete laws, such as those on parliamentary privilege, and should not "dig up old bones in the cemetery of obsolete and obsolescent laws".

All these writers agreed that, to put it bluntly, we pay our Judges to preserve the law of the land. We do not pay our Parliamentarians to do this. "The Law Courts do not invade Parliament, and Parliament has no right to invade the Courts."

**Letters, A D Kay.** Parliamentarians are the servants of the people, not their masters. They can be elected or rejected by the citizens, who pay their salaries and expect service.

For Parliament to gaol two of its masters, however unworthy, is to place the servant in the position of authority, which neither the Constitution allows nor the people desire.

The days of the Star Chamber belong to the dark and distant past.

# THE PRACTICE OF CHRISTIANITY

**Letters, G V S.** For 20 years I have resided in five different parts of the State. My home has always been located on a public street, in clear view and easy of access.

Never once, in those years, have we been visited by any clergyman, of any type or creed, for any purpose or reason.

Throughout my life I have been a consistent churchgoer when it has been physically possible. I would welcome any religious practitioner, no matter what his belief, provided he were honest.

Today, we cannot attend any local church services. The two miles of very rough road in this small country town are more than my wife can manage, and we have no car – or horse.

But no member of the clergy has ever offered to give us a lift, even on Christmas Day. So we have gone without (we have lived here five years).

No clergyman has called to ask who we are, what we are (matters which are irrelevant), or if we are in want.

I have made considerable inquiries in this and other towns, and have gathered the disturbing information that my case is not unusual.

**Comment**. This Letter reminds me that, until the mid-fifties, any family in a country town, or a city's suburbs, was generally greeted by three of four clergymen within the first week of residence. Their idea was to tell them that their own brand of faith was available somewhere nearby, and to add to their congregation.

Existing residents, whose religious preference was already known, were also visited at home about twice a year and urged to gain the blessing of church attendance. Hospitals, too, were good places to see collars.

Of course, from that time, it all changed, as the above Letter pointed out. Why was this so? Were the clergy getting lazy? Was the growth of secularism in society so strong that the clergy only mixed with the existing flock?

A few Letter-writers had their say on this.

**Letters, Clergyman, Sydney.** I must confess that G V S's Letter has stirred my conscience. I really must get on with the door-to-door visiting that would find out folk like him.

It is not made easier when I find that I must prepare addresses at the rate of 12 a week; that I have to teach Scripture to about 900 children each week; that, right now, there are folk in five different hospitals expecting a visit from me; that there is a list of sick and elderly folk, about 50 on it now, who expect to see me far more often than I find it possible to call; that funerals, only about two a week, can take up almost a whole afternoon; that there are five church organisations meeting weekly which demand a good deal of my time and help.

Editing and publishing a monthly paper is a chore with a merciless deadline.

For neglected correspondence and a garden screaming for attention I must stifle my conscience.

Even if I dared take it, Mr G V S's letter would spoil the day off we are always hoping might be possible. Any clergyman would want to help folk like G V S, and – like the doctor – **he is no further from him than the nearest telephone**.

**Letters, Non-Cleric.** G V S's letter would appear as a censure on the clergy; on the contrary it is a censure on the vast majority of nominal Christians who give no regard to religion, or extremely meagre support.

A glance at the statistics will show that it is utterly impossible for the few underpaid clergy (which contributing Christians are barely able to support) to visit each home even once in two or three years while carrying on their vital school instructions, hospital and manifold other duties.

Then, on such a rare visit, possibly the parishioner is absent!

Like G V S, the writer attends church, but has not been visited, nor expects he should be.

**Comment.** As correspondents made clear, the life of a clergyman was getting harder. The number of clergy in the nation was holding steady, but the population was booming from many births and from migration. On top of that, the number of Baptisms and Confirmations was at an all-time high, and all the other matters that the above writer mentioned were true. Little wonder that clergy had no time for house calls.

There was more to it than that, however. In a growing number of households, clergy were not welcome. Society was getting more and more secular, the belief in God was on the decline, and the sinful ways of the world were capturing new recruits every day. What clergyman wanted to call on a household and be faced with the one-sided arguments from an angry person who really had no knowledge of religion other than a bigotry instilled by other bigots? So, for one reason or another, the clergy were keeping themselves more and more to their own secure congregations.

## NEWS AND VIEWS

A family in Bundaberg, Queensland, has been blessed with the birth of **four healthy babies, now know as the Lucke Quads**. Everyone is healthy, and the father celebrated at the hospital by having **a few sandwiches** with reporters. No photographs are available because the Women's Weekly has exclusive rights.

# JULY NEWS ITEMS

July 5th. **Sanitary workers servicing 45,000 houses** in Sydney's southern suburbs **went on strike** for higher wages. Residents were advised by the authorities to bury nightsoil in their yards under at least eight inches of soil....

July 6th. Two large schools in the western and southern regions of Sydney have been shut down because of the strike by sanitary workers. **98,000 homes have now been affected, involving 400,000 persons. By the next day, the number of unsewered schools had grown to 56.** Authorities have warned of the spread of disease.

A lady in New York won $US32,000 (a small fortune) by **winning a quiz show**. Her questions were all about the Bible. One of the questions was to name the 12 Apostles. She will decide today if she will go on **for the $US64,000 question.** If she wins, **she will be the first contestant to do so.**

The National Union of Mine Workers **in Britain** reported that, last year, **371 miners were killed, 700 died from coal dust on the lungs, and 300,000 men** in the industry were partially disabled. Miners' leaders in Australia said that they understood that **the proportions here were the same**.

A Mrs Ruth Ellis **was executed in England** for **the shooting and killing of her boyfriend.** Since the beginning of the century, thirteen women have been executed in Britain, two in the last six months.

In Boorowa, a small farming town in NSW, a woman called Mrs Jones **is to be evicted from her Soldiers Settlement farm** by the Sheriff. She and her husband occupied the farm five years ago, but three years later he "shot through." This means that legally she must now leave the farm, and that decision was confirmed by the High Court this week....

She has **600 hundred merino sheep, and 30 head of cattle** and calves, two turkeys, two hens and three cattle dogs. She will not leave gracefully, and **will take to the road, droving the mob to who knows where**....

She lists among her virtues "**I can milk and shoe a horse**, and beat out a set of gate-hinges on the anvil. I can make wool rugs and bottle cauliflowers. I can make soup, do embroidery, and I built my back verandah." Her attitude is "OK, let 'em put me off. It'll probably take 'em days."

From July 11ᵗʰ, **Sydney's four newspapers**, normally hostile to each other, **have combined** to produce a single daily paper. They have done this because the members of the papers Unions are on strike....

This has all sorts of consequences but **the comic strips of the four papers are all there in every edition.** So on one page, you get V C Flint, Penny, Bluey and Curley, Joe Palooka, Dick Tracy, Martha Wayne, Juliet Jones, Roy Morgan M.D, Rip Kirby, Big Ben Bolt, The Potts, Dagwood and Mandrake.

# DOWN MEMORY LANE

At this time, I went back for a week to my home town in the Cessnock coalfields. It still had a population of 2,000 miners, and no one could suggest that it was a leader in anything. So, what a shock it was to find, as I walked round at dusk with my Dad, that the forces of change were rampaging through the centre of the shopping area, of four fallen-down shops.

First, we came to the blacksmith's. We all remembered Ben Enden, in a black singlet, shorts and pit boots, belting bits of glowing metal with a hammer, nailing shoes onto frightened horses, and beating the hell out of the panels from trucks and cars. Well, Ben had gone. Not only Ben, but the great big shed he worked in had gone, and the piles of junk he so lovingly played with were also gone. His block of land had been flattened by a dozer, and all that was left was a *FOR SALE* sign.

Next, the Butcher's shop in the Co-op. We pressed our noses to the window, and saw that all the sawdust had gone from the floor. That was silly. That shop always had an inch at least of fresh sawdust for catching blood from the dripping carcases. It was spread behind the counter in the area where the meat was cut up. If you asked for a pound of rump steak, Len would walk to a hanging carcase and cut it off for you. How could a butcher work without sawdust under him?

My Dad explained that the meat now was brought in already cut up, and Ben was gone and his place was taken by a retailer of cut meat. Who needs sawdust when there is no blood? It turned out that the meat now was not last-night's killing but instead was a week old, so **that it tasted as bad as today's meat**. Part of this, I was told, was that when you bought some, it was put into white semi-glossy paper, and not directly into the old newspapers of yesteryear. I could see how that would add to the difference.

Then to the School of Arts. The Library there was closed. How could they do this? For my last eight years of school, this was the very centre of my literary world. It had 30 volumes each of Perry Mason, Fu Man Chu, and William books. It had 300 volumes of Zane Gray, and other Westerns, it had stacks of Ethel M Dell and Pearl Buck for Mum. It was the place where the best literature in the world was exchanged. Now it was gone.

All of it was gone. The Fire Station was gone. The two petrol bowsers in front of the Store were gone. The silent cop to mark the right-hand turn away from the Store was gone. The horse water-troughs were gone. Was there anything left? Had the world changed so much in just a few years? I looked up the road and saw the Denman Hotel. It had been down-sized from four to two floors, but it was still there, and miracle though it might be, the doors were wide open, and the beer was on. We just had to verify that it really was still there; and indeed it was.

## DID I MENTION A SILENT COP?

I suppose you all remember what a silent cop is. It was a circle of metal, about a foot or more across, and some 5 inches high. It was often painted yellow, and was set into the roadway to mark places where vehicles did things.

In the days when a right-hand turn was signalled by waving gaily from the driver's window, these cops were useful to indicate the exact point where the turn should start from. So they were useful.

Some drivers thought they had some weaknesses.

**Letters, H J P Adams.** It is with anxiety that I view the manner in which "silent cops" are used at random in an attempt to ease the problem of traffic control.

One does not doubt the uses of a "silent cop" at intersections, but when three or four are used, they become a nuisance and a danger, particularly to low-slung and small cars.

This danger factor is increased further when the reflectors on them have been clogged up and no longer indicate the presence of the obstruction. In the wet, even those with reasonable reflectors are difficult to see.

If we must have "silent cops," and I do not claim we must not, then let them be fewer, let them be well placed, illuminated or iridescent and, finally, constructed in a resilient way so as to warn the offending motorist, but not crack his crankcase as a penalty for his hideous crime.

**Letters, E Gordon-Hume.** In the "Herald" of July 6, Mr H J P Adams drew attention to only two items of damage due to "silent cops."

The "two-decker," of which over 3,000 are in use in Sydney and suburbs, is nearly six inches in height. Due to its bad design, it causes damage to steering gear and tyres of motor vehicles by throwing them violently sideways.

That this happens often is proved by the fact that the yellow paint is ground off by the impact of the tyres, and has to be renewed frequently.

As Mr Adams pointed out, some are badly placed – one I know of is in the middle of a straight road, instead of in the side street.  The shadow of a tree falls on it during the morning, making it nearly invisible.  Running over it results in a nasty jar.  A double yellow line would answer the needs of the position.

Another caused the death of a motor cyclist in Waverley.

Such damage and the dangers mentioned will continue until an improved type – a flattened dome about four inches high, is substituted.

**Comment.**  In fact, it took a long time to actually remove all the silent cops across the nation. Last year, in South Australia, in a lazy country city, I saw quite a number still getting the annual coat of yellow paint.  But generally, they **started** to disappear about now, giving way to trafficators, glowing rear red lights, and new laws.

## MORE ON BYGONE DAYS

While I'm on the subject of our changing world, let me remind you that, back in 1955, the typical suburban or country town movie theatre generally had a fixed ritual for their audiences. They often started with a serial, then a B-grade movie, followed by an interval. After that, the trailers, a Tom and Jerry or Donald Duck, or a dreaded travelogue ("As the sun sinks slowly in the west...."), and then the main show of the week.  God Save the Queen, and it was all over till next week.

But, as we have recently discovered, change was everywhere. The two writers below wanted a simple change that would have suited them.

**Letters, Regular Saturday Nighter.** Why must the picture proprietors show the best picture at the end of the programme?

This means quite frequently that one has to sit through a mediocre film and several trailers before seeing the best part of the show.

Show the best first and give us a chance to get home early these cold nights.

**Letters, M J Holmes.** I am not a "Regular Saturday-nighter" at the cinema, but would be a "Regular Week-nighter" if only I could find a picture show where the feature film is always shown first.

Let picture-show managers "show the best first" and they will fill their now three-quarters empty theatres on week nights with: (1) The elderly and frail; (2) the workers who have to get up early next morning; (3) the parents who cannot afford baby-sitters till 11.30 but could ask a grandparent or neighbour to mind the baby till, say, 9.30; and (4) all who, like myself, get so cranky if they don't get eight hours' sleep that it just isn't worth going to the pictures.

**Comment.** It took a few years to come, and they got a change, but not the one they wanted. What happened was that the theatres cut out one film altogether, so that there was only one on the programme. A few years later, they went one further. They closed down most suburban and country theatres altogether. This, I hear, was because of the success of TV.

Still, about now, the American craze for drive-in movies came to Oz. But they're gone now too.

I will stop this memory-lane tour. I am getting morose.

## SHOULD CENOTAPHS BE REVERED?

Every city and town in the nation has some place where the dead from our various wars can be honoured. Often there is a brick memorial centre-piece with the names of the fallen printed on it, and perhaps places for flowers and flags. They are treated with respect on all days and, on special days of remembrance, they become the focus for a variety of commemorative functions.

Sydney has its own Cenotaph, right in the centre of the city, and fair and square in the heart of the business district. It is bounded on one side by George Street, and on the other by Pitt Street. Its neighbours are the head office of the Commonwealth Bank and the Sydney GPO. So, the roads approaching it are full of pedestrians and shoppers, and trams and buses and cars. This makes the following correspondence all the more interesting.

**Letters, T Urban, Gloucestershire, England.** I have just returned to England after a splendid trip to Australia. The one thing that disappointed me was the casual attitude of your people towards the remembrance of the many fine men who gave their lives and their bodies towards protecting your country from enemies in many wars.

It was most noticeable in Sydney where the excellent Cenotaph is beautifully presented, right in the centre of the city. Business goes on all around it, as the people flow about doing their jobs.

But it is rare to see some passer-by acknowledge the fallen heroes. People talk and giggle as they pass, nary a hat is raised, no one bows even one bit. It is just like any other monument to almost all the population.

It is all very well to say that, on special days, they will have a proper deferential attitude. But I hold that every day is special when it comes to remembering our dead soldiers. Respect for the dead is not something that you can turn on for two or three days a year.

I shudder to think that it might take some government ordinance to enforce a respectable attitude, but I can see no alternative.

**Letters, Tom Roberts.** I remember my fallen mates at two times during the year. **One of these** is every second night when I wake from a nightmare that recalls the night in a Jap prison camp when they finally cut my arm off.

**The second** is more voluntary of my part when, about twice a year, I take a bottle of cheap whisky and go to a small nook on the edge of Lake Macquarie. I sit and remember the lingering deaths of 20 of my near-mates over three years, and the deaths of 50 others more remote. I have plenty of memories.

The point is that I do not want anyone else to share this with me. I have my own way, and time, of remembering, and you can have yours. But don't try to make me take my hat off at some time and place of your choosing.

Proper contemplation and remembrance can't be regulated.

**Letters, Peter Olsen.** I am a messenger for a big bank in Martin Place. I go past the Cenotaph a dozen or more times a day. Should I doff my hat every time? In both directions?

Should cars and taxis sound their horns? Should bus and tram passengers all stand up as they pass?

Suppose you answer yes to these questions, and suppose that everyone does as I suggested they might. Will it make one jot of difference to anything?

## THE END OF THE PAPER STRIKE

I mentioned earlier that workers at the four Sydney dailies went on strike for, as usual, better wages and conditions. The four papers combined together to produce a composite paper, and that allowed them to keep the flow of news going. After a week or so, the workers went back to work, and as happened ten years earlier, part of the cease-fire agreement was that **the papers would not editorialise against the workers**. That is, they would not use their editorial power to bore it up the strikers, and would instead make no reference to the evils of the strike.

The papers stuck to their word. They were, in general, quite restrained, and ceased their coverage and commentary on the strike. But the *SMH*, **on the first day after the strike**, did let **the first two letters** slip through. They were not at all addressing the strike. **No, No. They would not do that.** Yet they seemed to somehow point out that strikes, and governments that did nothing to control strikers, were not good for the country.

**Letters, Eric F Moore.** The recent strikes, newspapers, gas, buses, etc., are nothing new to the unfortunate residents of this State or country. It is possible that a country not so well endowed by nature, as Australia, could not exist with all the upsets we experience.

Strikes are apparently our normal way of life. The right to strike appears to be far more important than the right to work.

During recent years, all kinds of complicated machinery has been created to prevent strikes. Both State and Federal Governments, at considerable cost to the taxpayer, have instituted these tribunals. Are they worthwhile?

It is of very little interest to read that Mr Justice or Conciliation Commissioner so and so will review the matter in a few days.

It is just possible that, when this country grows up, they may arrive at some scheme, at no cost to the taxpayer, whereby the employers and employees of a certain industry may get together, draw up a contract of work, binding on both parties, for a certain period, with suitable, individual penalties for any persons who break the agreement.

**Letters, Carbolic.** As one who believes that the only hope of mankind, here or hereafter, lies in the rule of Christ, I am no admirer or follower of either Right or Left in the buck-passing democracy to which we have devolved.

But I cannot but express my indignation at the gross inconsistencies manifested by the present NSW Government.

On the one hand we observe the law invoked to dispossess a lone but worthy and hardworking woman from her well-run farm solely on a hair-splitting legal technicality.

But on the other hand the repeated protests of responsible citizens against breaches of law involving serious moral issues are ignored. Like Gallilio, the NSW Government "cares nothing for these things."

The cowardly inactivity of the Government in the face of the present wave of strikes, all of which have been duly pronounced "unlawful", contrasts most horribly with the brave and holy determination of Mr Cahill and his followers to grind the face of Mrs Jones, of Boorowa, in the dust.

One is driven to the conclusion that if she only had 10,000 votes she, too, would be immune from the operation of the law.

My compliments to Mr Cahill on his sardonic humour in appointing Mr Landa "to watch" the progress of the present unlawful strike of nightsoilmen, but again, to those who have any nose for moral issues, this only serves to demonstrate that there is an awful smell in Macquarie Street.

**Comment.** I leave it to you to decide if they were close to the wind. Would the ex-strikers say that the *SMH* had violated the no-comment clause of the agreement? It must have been a close call.

## HERALDRY IN FASHION

By the time I left high school in the early fifties, that august place was talking about having its own Coat of Arms. We had cited a motto for years that said, not very originally, "What e'er you do, do well". Now, it was thought that some sort of scholastic improvement could be achieved if we added **a coat of arms**, and so various artists were busy drawing kangaroos and wombats in a bid to satisfy the selectors.

This scene was repeated all over Australia. The early fifties was indeed the Age of Heraldry in Oz, as people, including schools and golf clubs, sought to guarantee their place in history.

There were, however, some cautious voices

**Letters, G A Dillon.** Your special correspondent deserves wide approval for bringing to notice in your Educational Supplement the facts in regard to school arms, as displayed on note-paper, blazers, ties, etc.

Recently I sent a specimen illustration of one of these coats of arms to one of the Heralds at the College of Arms (London). This one had been assumed by a private school of some standing here in Australia. The Herald, in reply, admitted that the achievement was indeed a kind of heraldry, but a very peculiar kind.

Need I add that such arms had, of course, never been sanctioned for use by the College of Arms. Even if that school could produce the necessary fee – 105 Pounds – for a grant of arms, their existing coat would be subject to considerable rectification.

I wonder how many schools in Australia are actually making use of bogus arms. In England their number is considerable, too.

It was only within the last 20 years or so that the arms of Harrow and Rugby were approved by the College of Arms, and then after some rectification.

I once spoke to an Australian headmaster on the subject of his (school) arms. He admitted that they were assumed without authority and added, by way of explanation, "Of course 'they' do not understand that kind of thing." "They" were the school council, and the kind of thing they did not understand was – heraldry.

I hesitated to rejoin that only one remove from bogus arms was a bogus degree, but personally I consider that they are just about on the same level. Perhaps I am old fashioned.

**Letters, W K Wood.** It is evident that there are many people who do not care a scrap whether coats of arms are "bogus" or otherwise.

Naturally, the Heralds at the College of Arms (London) are anxious to perpetuate a situation which gives them some importance but really, the whole thing is childish.

To the devil with silly codes and systems of behaviour that put mankind's brain in a strait-jacket!

**Comment.** There was a cost to getting a properly authorised Coat of Arms. There was an initial cost, and then an annual fee. As this became more widely known, the passion for getting a proper one diminished.

At the same time, people began to look down their noses at the amateur designs and ornamentation. In any case, we ran out of kangaroos willing to pose. The craze died out in a few years.

## NEWS AND VIEWS

**The first shipment of uranium oxide ore** was dispatched today **to the US** from Rum Jungle. The uranium was sent under a contract that will last for ten years.

**Rice is now back on the Australian menu**, at last. Many of **you will remember rice puddings**. However, **do you remember sago? Can you send me your Mum's recipe for sago pudding?** I want to see if I still hate it.

**Princess Margaret will turn 25 on August 21st**. Observers are still asking **if she will marry Captain Peter Townsend**.

Last year, Australia lost **the Davis Cup. It has just taken it back** when Lew Hoad and Rex Hartwig won the doubles, to take an unbeatable lead 3-0 in the Series.

A Texas housewife just won **a new Dodge car every year for the rest of her life** on a TV quiz show.

Strikes are so numerous that I do not report on most of them. I will make an exception to tell you that **50 gravediggers in Sydney are now on strike** for, guess what, higher wages. So far their action, or inaction, has delayed 100 funerals.

# AUGUST NEWS ITEMS

The influential British medical journal, *Practitioner*, argued that **the stress of a large wedding**, and then an over-planned and over-vaunted honeymoon, **were bad for a marriage**....

"The sheer fatigue of the wedding day is accentuated by the current social customs of having an **elaborate wedding ceremony, followed by an elaborate reception**. Is there any good reason why the bride and groom should be exposed to this entirely unnecessary strain?"....

"There would appear to be good medical grounds for replacing **these gargantuan celebrations** by a simple ceremony, religious or civil, followed **by an informal lunch with relatives and friends – after the honeymoon**." What would *Practitioner* say about today's weddings?

Sydney's *Sun Herald* promises **weekend reading that should thrill the nation**. It says that recently found **letters from Marie-Louise**, the wife of Napoleon Bonaparte, will be published and they "are loving, vivid, complaining, telling in the same breath of a girl's deeply personal feelings and of Europe-shaking events"....

**Letters from Napoleon will also be published.** "The exultation of a conqueror, fading into the despair of a beaten dictator". **Comment**: Given that it will be as absorbing as "a historical romance, and as intimate as yesterday," **it should be well worth the four pence**.

This year's **round-Australia Redex car reliability trial** will start on **Sunday** August 21st from Parramatta Park (Sydney). There will be about 200 starters, and interest across the nation is still very high. **The trial will take three weeks** and will end back at Parramatta Park. **This year, the emphasis will be on the reliability of the cars, and not on speed. Maybe.**

This trial was not expected to be as wild and woolly as earlier trials, because **the cars can readily reach their destinations in the time allotted**. Still, over the next few days the following headlines were seen:

*Redex cars in fast night race.*

*Horror day for Redex cars.*

*"Somebody will be killed in Redex."*

*Car wrecks strew horror road.*

*Redex nightmare.*

All of these were published in the first five days of the trial. There was lots of good reading to come.

Senior Army officials are alarmed about **the low number of recruits for the Army**. They offer all sorts of excuses: the lessening of international tension, the ready availability of jobs, and the attractive pay rates for unskilled workers....

**They would be more realistic** if they said that they will be **used as front-line troops against terrorists in Malaya**, and that is not a pleasant prospect for any **well-balanced** lad.

## DESIGNING THE SYDNEY OPERA HOUSE

Sydney's Opera House is now recognised world-wide as a magnificent piece of architecture. It is sometimes described, quite foolishly, as the eighth wonder of the world. But it is pretty good, and now that it is built and has been in operation for decades, can also be said to be standing the test of time.

Early on though, and all through its construction, there was no certainty that it would be as successful as it now is. Right from the very beginning, controversy dogged it at every stage. As a current example, I will dig into one aspect at its very beginning, namely, who was to design the structure?

Public correspondence on this matter was kicked off by a Mr Roy Grounds, an Australian architect currently domiciled in Rome. There had been suggestions that an architectural competition should be called for, and invitees should submit their design, and that the best should be selected. Mr Grounds was not in favour of this, and instead suggested that **a panel of judges should be anointed**, and that it then invite architects from round the world to submit designs. He suggested seven names for this panel, and none of them were Australian, though he did add:

> Post-war Europe, with its vast rebuilding programme, has been the proving ground for this procedure. Its adoption in Australia for the Sydney Opera House should insure against a repetition of the sorry fiasco of Melbourne's Western Market and Olympic Stadium competitions, and result in a building worthy of what must be the finest site for its purpose in the world.

This Letter seemed to be saying that Australians would not be up to the task, and it brought a vigorous response to the charge. It also, inter alia, provided a summary of some of the logistics of running an international competition.

Professor F Towndrow, of the Architecture Department of the NSW University of Technology, rallied to the rescue of our local lads. He first of all took issue with a Letter by a Mr Grounds' suggestion who said that Australian architects were mediocre. Not so, replied Towndrow. There is no evidence whatsoever to suggest such a charge.

In fact, Towndrow and others went on to say that after recent overseas visits, they were convinced that fully-qualified Australian architects were as good or better than any they had seen overseas. Granted, the locals did not have the same opportunities as Europeans, because there were many grand projects under way **there**. But the end result was that Australian architects were of first-class standard and would no doubt rise to the challenge if given a chance.

Suppose we were foolish enough to open the project to competition from overseas. Maybe it might be hoped that someone with recent experience in designing and building an opera house would apply.

Not likely, said Towndrow and the others. First of all, this applicant would be too busy on his own projects to bother with another one. Or he might be so rarified that he would in fact be **on the panel** that made the final choice, and thus be debarred from entering.

Then there was the cost of freighting the many drawings and reports backwards and forwards to Europe. The cost of this, and its administration, would deter applicants. On top of this, any decent applicant would need to come to Australia for interviews and discussion. Or, the selection panel would need to go to Europe. In either case, the cost would be enormous.

But why make it international in the first place? We **could** make a **gesture** by allowing interstate applicants to submit a proposal, but that surely would be enough. We would probably get about 500 entries, and that in itself would involve an enormous amount of work for the judges.

Towndrow concludes that "Surely amongst these 500, one Australian will be found of outstanding ability who, even if he has never previously designed an opera house, can do just what any overseas winner would do; and that is, get the consulting assistance of some expert in the field. And an Australian would have the added advantage of being wise to our local and peculiar conditions in Labor and materials."

**Letters, Walter Bunning.** Few established architects in other countries would be physically able to carry on their own practice in their own country and at the same time give personal "on-the-spot" attention to this enormous project. Any other arrangement for collaboration with a local firm must inevitably fail.

**Letters, George Molnar.** Since 1952, many new theatres have been built or are being built in Germany, Austria, Italy and USA. Many of them, like the theatres in Kassel, Bohum, Mannheim, were the result of competitions – in the case of Mannheim, an international competition.

It would be foolish and irresponsible not to take advantage of the accumulated knowledge of overseas experiences which would be made available to us by an international competition.

To have a restricted competition would be displaying the very sign of inferiority complex of which Professor Towndrow accuses Mr Grounds. To say we are as good as or even better than anybody else, yet to object to this being put to the test, is not a sign of either courage or confidence.

Professor Towndrow reckons on 500 entries from Australia alone. I doubt this figure. There were about 20 entries for the Olympic stadium, with all its nationwide publicity – only 70 for the swimming pool. This was at a time of comparative slackness. With the present buoyant state of the building industry, there will be fewer architects with the time to spare on such a more complex project.

Despite what Professor Towndrow has written I still firmly believe that the practice of our universities in making their appointments on a competitive basis from **all over the British Empire**, instead of restricting them to NSW, still results in our getting the best people for professors.

**Letters, Margaret Senior.** How will Australia ever develop its long-retarded, indigenous architecture if **the few luscious plums** of opportunity go to designers remote from here.

The design for our Opera House is going to cause endless controversy whoever becomes responsible for it. Public response will be the warmer towards a project we can feel is wholly ours, as it should be. If the selectors are wise, we need not fear the worst.

**Letters, G Molnar.** There is no justification for saying that an international competition would add at least nine months to the time needed for a national competition. All information on local conditions must be part of the conditions of competition, be it national or international. Rolled up drawings can reach

Australia from anywhere in the world in a week; air freight costs no more than mounting of drawings for local competitions.

**Letters, Diana Phipps.** Professor Towndrow, writing about the Opera House competition, worries about the high cost of air freight of competition designs for overseas competitors.

Mr Bunning worries about the difficulty of overseas competitors supervising the building of the Opera House in Sydney.

Both suggest that the best way **to overcome these difficulties is to bar them** from entering the competition.

We think we have reached world standard in architecture. We think we have reached world standard in tennis.

The Australian tennis championship is open to all-comers; it results in pretty good tennis and Australians sometimes win it. Could our architects not show the same spirit of sportsmanship, if they are so confident of the standard they have achieved?

**First Comment.** You can see how the correspondence touched on strong emotions. After this, **at every stage**, emotions just as strong were aroused.

**Second comment.** Do you remember who the ultimate designer was? Was he an Australian?

# CHURCHES LAGGING THE COMMUNITY?

**Letter, Hopeful Christian.** I have just read the weekend sermons from three leading clergymen. The first talked about how death is just the beginning. The second came up with the Parable of the Sower which pushes the idea of predestination. The third advocates falling back (somehow) on Jesus Christ when the pressure gets to us.

Church-goers will recognise these messages as being similar to those given to them all their lives. Some people will be happy with them, but others, in increasing numbers, are saying that they are tired of the same old message, and that they themselves could get up and give exactly the same epistle.

They are adding that such messages are avoiding all the current issues of today. What really should be our attitude to Communism in nations overseas; should we trade with them, should we join industry groups that are seeking to reduce their influence in the Unions? There are a multitude of issues, like the Aborigines, National Service for young men, water for inland Australia, for example, that need comment and Christian guidance.

Where can that Christian guidance come from if it does not come from the pulpit? Yet the churches persist in the abstruse and heads-in-the–sands sermons like those given above. No wonder, most people are saying, that the churches are losing their influence and that, as a consequence, standards in the community are falling.

## REDEX TRIAL CONTINUES

The Trial went on its merry way. Day after day the number of cars was reduced, drivers were trapped under overturned vehicles, broken ribs reported to hospitals, wombats were slaughtered, and innocent vehicles were run off the road. It all made good reading from afar, but serious minded people were asking whether such a race could ever be turned into **a reliability trial** instead of the **initial concept of a good old speed trial**.

A few Letters show mixed of support for the event.

**Letters, A F Parkinson, Secretary, Road Safety Council of NSW.** In spite of the warnings against speeding by the Police Superintendent of Traffic, Mr Gribble, the Redex motor trial has developed into another mad race.

The apparent lack of action in respect of the rocket speeds outside the built-up areas is perhaps due to the heart-breaking impossibility of proving to the Courts that these deadly speeds are, in the words of the prima facie rule, "dangerous to the public in the circumstances existing at the time."

The police could, nevertheless, confound these drivers with the regulation prohibiting racing on the public roads and highways.

If the Redex trial serves no other useful purpose, it should at least convince Australians, faced with a staggering and increasing toll of the road, of the desperate need for the rigid control of speed and the consistent and impartial enforcement of the life-giving traffic laws.

**Letters, John F Crouch.** Mr Parkinson no doubt expresses the horse-and-buggy outlook of a few citizens who would condemn competitive motor trials that naturally assist in the economic development of our great country.

Road safety workers and the police know only too well that the bullock tracks that serve as our present-day roads are taking a heavy toll on the lives of all people in our community.

From the past two Redex Trials have come numerous improvements to our locally made and imported cars, making for greater safety. Our roads, bridges, creek crossings, etc., have also been greatly improved.

To condemn this international motor competition as a "mad race" reflects nothing but an archaic outlook.

**Letters, Hugh Allen.** One is not surprised to read that speeds of 90 miles an hour were reached on occasions in the Redex trial to date in order to average the 47 miles per hour over specified distance.

The fact that missiles have been thrown at the contestants at various points, suggests that the Redex trial does not meet with general approval or is pure vandalism.

Most Australians like contests of various kinds – especially where an element of risk is attached – but don't allow such risks to be in contrast with the traffic laws as we understand them.

As an old motorist of many years standing, in which I have contested and won hill climbs, etc., I can see nothing in this present Redex trial with absurd mileage rates over good, bad and indifferent roads – other than a publicity stunt on the part of the motor trade at the possible expense of good Australian motorists' lives.

My personal feeling is that this event will be the last Redex trial on such lines. Something more rational will eventuate which will help a good motor car and a capable but not a fool driver to win the contest.

**Letters, W R McLean.** As it stands, the Redex trial favours the big car. I suggest that, instead of running the trial as an open event, it be conducted along the lines of the grand Prix, and a formula adopted, with correspondingly higher speeds (but reasonable speeds) for the various classes.

These classes should be decided by engine capacity.

By conducting the trial in this manner and reducing average speeds, the trial would be made safer and more interesting, and car manufacturers would be provided with an incentive to design sturdier and more economical cars with higher performance engines and increased driver comfort.

**Letters, Thomas D Esplin.** The Redex trial once again is proving that there are many cars, quite suitable for city driving, or normal country touring, which, by overloading and overdriving, can be knocked about on "horror" stretches.

Many people, who live where such "horror" stretches are normal, use jeeps, utilities, or vehicles with four-wheel drive, yet these are excluded from the Redex trial by the regulations. I suggest that next year – and every alternate year thereafter – **the Redex trial be confined exclusively to utilities, jeeps, four-wheel vehicles, and cars towing trailers.**

The information gained would be of great value to the man on the land.

**Comment.** When the Trials started a few years ago, most people were excited and the first Trial was an all-consuming spectator-sport success. You can see from the above that this enthusiasm is waning given the toll that the event is taking on roads and bridges, animals, fences, and even humans. It was inevitable that at some time human lives would be lost, and the results were such that it was hard to see **whether** a particular vehicle was most suited to the conditions, or whether the prize winners were the teams that were the best at bending the rules. Over the next few years, the rules were gradually tightened so that the excesses were reduced. When this happened, interest was reduced, and the contest lost its mass appeal.

## ONE-MAN BUSES

By the end of the month, the NSW State Government had introduced one-man buses on some City-of-Sydney routes.

Over the course of the month, the pros and cons of these buses had been argued back and forth and of course, no one had changed their initial opinion.

On this matter, I will just give you a sample that consists of the last two Letters before the Editor of the *SMH* closed the correspondence.

**Letters, W H Steel.** As run in Sydney, one-man buses are both slow and uncomfortable. With the present method of collecting fares and giving tickets and change, it may take 10 minutes to fill the bus while the use of only one door for both entering and alighting can mean an uncomfortable struggle to descend, and more delay before other passengers can enter.

**Letters, Andrew Wilson.** I do agree that operators in Britain do use large one-man buses, but only on express and private hire, a totally different class of operation altogether.

Certainly other countries use one-man buses, such as Canada and America, but the paying system is very different: "Nickel-in-the-slot."

**Comment.** You can bet that there is more to come on this issue.

## NEWS AND VIEWS

The NSW Bushfire Committee issued a warning that bushfires would again be prevalent this season. It included **the normal urgings to build fire-breaks, and to keep house gutters free from leaves**. It added that "householders can increase their safety margin by keeping **a knapsack spray or pump or a rake and shovel handy**."

**Comment.** Bushfires must have been more easily tamed in those days.

## SEPTEMBER NEWS ITEMS

A new trouble spot is appearing on the world map. **Egypt and Israel**, always ready to clash with each other, have started a series of **shove and counter-shove on their border**. This will escalate and become important next year in **the so-called Suez crisis**. The current displays of animosity are **just lead-ins to that big main event.**

When the **leading cars in the Redex trial reached Melbourne, 200,000 people were cheering cars** as they arrived at the check-point.

**At mid-night** on the same day, a **crowd of 200 people cheered as Fitzgerald and Browne were released from Goulbourn goal** at the end of their three-month sentence, courtesy of the Federal Parliament.

Britain will conduct **testing of atomic devices in Austra**lia in a few months. Australia will share in the tests. They will be at Monte Bello Islands off our the north-west coast, and then at Maralinga, 500 mile West of Woomera in South Australia. **It is expected that there will be strident opposition to the tests**, despite the Government's assurance that there will be no danger to the population.

**The end of the Redex trial was very confusing**. The provisional winners were not confirmed because it was alleged that their engines had cracks in them, **Gelignite Jack Murray was disqualified** because at Sydney he drove home instead of to the check-point, at Canberra on the final leg a third of the field was directed **into a**

**bog by a bogus policeman**, and the Ball to celebrate the winners was left with **no winners yet declared**.

**The Royal Commission into Soviet espionage in Australia handed down its recommendations.** It found that Soviet spying in Australia had occurred, and while not seen as dangerous in the past, had implications for the future. **No person was to be charged for any breaches of the law.** Some laws might be changed to give us greater protection.

**Argentina's President, General Peron, often described as a dictator in the worst sense of the word, has been deposed. He and his wife, Eva, have fled the country**....

Most readers will remember that Peron's wife Eva was immortalised by the **popular musical** Evita. Remember the song *Don't Cry for me Argentina*....

An Italian sculptor is left with a statue, almost completed, of Peron. It was to have **weighed 43,000 tons, and stood 450 feet high, in white marble**. That was 150 feet higher that the US Statue of Liberty. Now, it seems to be of little value.

News item, September 25th. **The US President, Eisenhower, suffered a heart attack.** He was **diagnosed with coronary thrombosis, with no after-effects**, though he will have to rest for several weeks.

The President of the NSW Graziers' Association said **that over 100,000 sheep were stolen every year in the State of NSW alone.**

**Comment. That's a lot of sheep.**

# HOW SACRED ARE SUNDAYS?

It was now 10 years since the war finished. During the war, many people turned to the churches for solace and prayer, which caused attendance to swell, and meant that people were more inclined to listen to the clergy. Since then, the world had dropped more and more of the old strictures that the path to the Kingdom of God imposed on them, and questions were being asked everywhere about what good old-fashioned restrictions and practices actually did.

One question that kept popping up concerned **Sunday sport**. Was Sunday sport a violation of God's law to keep holy the Sabbath Day? And if it was allowed, was it acceptable to commercialise it by asking patrons to pay to watch it? Then, a spin-off was whether the money could rightly be used only for the benefit of sporting clubs, **or** could it go to entrepreneurs trying to make profits? Were large crowds shouting and barracking at matches consistent with God's will for Sundays?

One Letter on the subject, early in the month, did not get a single response.

**Letters, (Rev) Ivan Stebbins.** Last Monday the "Herald" published a picture of a crowd of more than 20,000 at a Sunday football match in Sydney, and also mentioned the gate money.

I have been surprised at no protest from the Churches. Has the command, "Remember the Sabbath day to keep it holy," lost its ancient sanction on the Churches as well as the community? Has the holy day become a wild holiday?

I fear that the **substitution of morning classes** for afternoon Sunday schools of most Protestant Churches has loosed a vast potential for these Sunday crowds.

One of the largest of our Churches, a generation ago, frowned on organised sport on Sundays. Now it not only condones it, but organises Sunday sport itself. Is the ancient claim of "semper ideam" still applicable to that Church?

Then, a later Letter brought out interested parties.

**Letters, Alan Walker, Mission to the Nation.** I criticised the launching of the Redex trial on Sunday because it was a vivid example of the way the day is gradually being taken over by commercial, sporting and political interests.

The fact is that we, as Australians, need to re-think the whole question of the Christian Sunday. Few of us would desire any return to a strict Puritan Sabbath, but I am convinced large numbers of Australians are completely opposed to the commercialisation of the day and are prepared to take a stand for the preservation of its Christian values.

Freedom of worship surely means freedom **to** worship. The social pressures which begin to operate virtually deny people, especially young people, freedom to worship. Likewise the commercialisation of Sunday obviously increases the number who must work to transport and feed large crowds of people.

Surely we should be eager to preserve for each other as far as possible freedom from work, the possibility of family unity and the opportunity for Sunday worship.

Of course, the whole issue comes back to a question of values. If Christian worship is of no importance, if the training of children in Christian citizenship is a waste of time, then, without protest, commercial interests such as represented by the Redex organisers will be permitted to encroach further and further into Sunday.

There is, however, another point of view: It is that the Christian Sunday has meant so much to us as a people that it is worth struggling to stop it being turned gradually into just another day of the week.

Reverend Alan Walker was a well-known defender of conservative religion, and his views were always well received by his flock. But there were other views.

**Letters, (Mrs) Ruth Jarvi.** This "gloomy Sunday" business makes many new migrants, especially when they are absolutely alone, very unhappy.

Speaking from my own experience, I can say that I used to fear the approaching weekend when I first arrived, and since have spoken with migrants from different countries. We all completely agreed that Sunday was the day when we got really homesick.

**Letters, Payten Lewis.** I was delighted to read your editorial in answer to the outburst by the Rev Alan Walker over the crowds who went forth on Sunday to see the Redex trial cars take off.

Surely it is time we had a more realistic approach to the gloomy Sunday.

If I could feel for one moment that we were on a higher spiritual plane than London with its open cinemas on Sunday afternoon, then there might be an excuse for the dull Sunday inflicted on a city the size of Sydney.

**Letters, (Rev) T P McEvoy.** Your correspondent, Mrs Jarvi, and other migrants whose views she expresses, will glean little comfort from the thought that here in Australia among the greatest opponents of Sunday shows are the employees engaged in show business.

Moreover, why should the principle of a day of rest be violated in the interests of play-goers any more than in the interests of housewives and others who, at great inconvenience to themselves, lay in a weekend stock of provisions in order that butcher, baker, grocer and others may enjoy the long weekend?

Worship and rest, as distinct from recreation, were its salient features and where these were accepted by the people they proved to be a moral discipline of inestimable value, not to speak of the physical boon accruing therefrom.

**Letters, Christian.** The truly sincere church-goers will attend church whether there is sport or not. But in this democratic community let us, as citizens, have the right to Sunday entertainment, just as ministers have the right to conduct services on a week-day.

**Letters, (Rev) J H Somerville.** The most noticeable thing about the letters of those who favour a "Continental" Sunday is the complete absence of any reference to the Divine Will as expressed in the fourth Commandment of the Moral Law.

One would think the observance of a weekly day of rest from work was merely a man-made law, and not a definite command of God.

The Ten Commandments are the fundamental laws of physical health as well as of soul health.

**Letters, (Rev) R W Hemming; (Rev) G J Ward .** So the Redex trial emerges as a farce. We are not surprised because it began and ended with a considered and deliberate act of corporate insult to Almighty God in the desecration of the Lord's Day.

Of course when the Laws of God are set aside it is not long before the laws of man are ignored. The instructions of the Chief Secretary as to the conditions governing organised sport on Sundays were completely ignored, indeed we doubt whether any approach was made to him for permission to stage the Redex trial on Sundays.

It ought not be overlooked that the farce was so nearly a tragedy when some competitors admitted that when faced with death by thirst, they prayed to the God whom they had insulted, and He of His mercy heard their prayer.

**Comment.** I do not need to tell you that the battle over sport and gates on Sunday is well and truly over, nor do I need to say who won. Likewise, for Sunday trading in shops, pubs, petrol stations, movie theatres, ocean cruises, Sunday markets and many other enterprises. I will not try to work out whether it is in fact a good thing, but if you go by the numbers of people who participate in Sunday events, then most of the community endorses the changes.

## RED FACES FOR THE AIR FORCE

On September 1st, a small Auster aircraft accidentally took off from Bankstown airport near Sydney without a pilot. It flew in a circle over Sydney suburbs and out to sea, and because it might crash into a suburb, the Civil Aviation authorities requested the Air Force to shoot it down when it passed over the ocean.

The Air Force responded with a Sabre fighter which tracked the plane to ensure there was no small child aboard, and then fired on the craft. However, its gun jammed, and the plane did another circuit. The Army then called on the Navy to do the job, and the Navy was able to oblige.

The Air Force pointed out that it was such a trivial matter that it did not alert its fighter planes at Williamtown. "You do not take a 12-inch gun to shoot a mouse." It also said that its airmen at Richmond were on stand-down, in peace time.

Still, this did not stop the critics from laying in the boot.

**Letters, A McD Knowles.** As a returned soldier, I am greatly alarmed at the unpreparedness exhibited by the RAAF concerning their attempted shooting down of the runaway Auster aircraft.

I am further astounded at the excuse by the Minister for Air, Mr Townley, for the RAAF not having available armed aircraft capable of destroying the plane.

It would appear that Mr Townley expects an intending enemy to give us notice of an attack in order that our Air Force may be alerted.

The Navy is to be commended in so far as it went about the job in a business-like fashion with two properly equipped planes.

**Letters, R Jackson.** The "little comedy of the Auster" could indeed be well worth the 3,000 Pounds loss if the red faces and hung heads in the RAAF help to bring the Prime Minister to the realisation of the need for civil defence.

It also highlighted the fact that Mr W C Wentworth was once again on the ball and is, as has been clearly demonstrated in the past, that rather rare animal, a politician with foresight.

**Letters, Ex-Army Tobruk Rat**. The Air Minister's excuse for the RAAF not being able to deal with the runaway Auster was that it was on a "peacetime" footing. Surely he must be aware that there will be no nice sporting declaration of war next time.

RAAF training should be directed towards repelling shock attacks on our main cities and strategic targets within minutes. Witness the speed with which the Americans and Russians deal with unidentified planes.

# THE SIZE OF CITIES

The Catholic Bishops' annual conference this year advocated smaller cities. Not that they expected the size of existing cities to reduce, they just wanted them to not increase, and they wanted no more cities in the future to rival Sydney and Melbourne in size.

Of course, what they wanted would be hard to achieve. Put simply, the jobs and facilities were already in the cities, and that attracted people. As our young people became more mobile, as they did about this time, it was like moths to the candle. But also, Governments poured money into their major cities, prices were cheaper there, and if you wanted something that was scarce, the city was the place to track it down.

Beyond that, the infrastructure cost of building in a city is much smaller than building towns for the same number of people. Take water pipes as an example. To lay pipes for city dwellers is a fraction of the cost of laying them for a sprawled-out town.

Still, the Bishops' proposal got mixed support.

**Letters, John A McCallum.** The Roman Catholic Bishops' proposal to limit the size of our great cities merits the support not only of their own adherents but also of those who do not generally look to them for guidance.

The concentration of industry, financial direction, higher education and administration in the State capitals has produced many evils.

It wastes a large part of people's lives in unnecessary and unpleasant travelling; it robs many children of "happy play in grassy places" (R L Stevenson's recipe for wisdom and strength); it encourages the surrender of individuality to herd impulses.

That most people will live in towns is inevitable. Only a small minority can live on isolated farms or small villages. But the ideal city should be much smaller than Sydney or Melbourne and should have large areas of parks reserved for recreation and rest.

To build such cities rather than crowd more and more people into our State capitals should be the positive aim of Governments and controllers of industry.

**Letters, Malcolm Fraser.** I agree with the Roman Catholic Bishops who deprecate the crowding of Australia's population into a few capital cities along a highly vulnerable coastline.

However, they should set a good example themselves by abandoning their site at Mona Vale for a Catholic university. Somewhere near Katoomba or Cooma would be ideal.

**Letters, Michael Sawtell.** We must have **some** large cities for industrial mass production, but **too many large cities will spell the ruin of any civilisation.**

Civilisation exists to give large numbers of people opportunities and encouragement to acquire culture, but how is all this possible unless men at some time in their lives, have lived close to Mother Earth and experienced the miracle that we call Nature?

**Letters, R Close.** Every Government in this nation, whether Federal or State, is spending the bulk of its money in the cities. Not just on the people there, but on building infrastructure, amenities, and Departments as well.

Look at the budget and you will see what I mean. Every local Council outside the city is on a shoestring compared to similar Councils in the city.

The private sector tries sometimes to build outside the major cities. But they are frustrated because all the decision making at the government level is done in cities, and is done with the eyes of a city dweller.

With money and power going to the cities, would any ambitious young man want to live in the country? Would any young girl stay in the country when all the ambitious young men are going to the cities?

I live in a suburb, a posh suburb, in Sydney. I would like to live in the country again. But I won't. I am old, and decrepit, and need the best hospital services at times. I can only get them in the city. I need to fight with government departments over all sorts of things. Can I do that by letter from the country? Don't be silly.

It all adds up. The cities are here to stay. Not only that, they will get bigger and bigger.

**Letters, John A McCallum, The Senate, Canberra.** When I wrote, It meant that we should build up cities, **other than Sydney**, with the goals of an optimum size and a rational plan always in our mind.

All we can do with Sydney now is to replace slums by flats with some recreational ground nearby, preserve and enlarge our areas of parks, improve our means of communication and induce those to whom the metropolis is an irresistible magnet to live in satellite towns.

While I believe our rural population should be increased, my plea was mainly for a good urban life in cities sufficiently large to provide the cultural advantages which are necessarily lacking in purely rural areas.

I want a better distribution of urban population, not a return to a peasant economy. I want Armidale, Orange, Wagga and other towns to become "ideal cities."

**Comment.** In 1955 it might have been possible to stop the drift, and then the flight, to the city. In the war, many factories had been moved to the country to alleviate the dangers of bombings. Some of the population followed it, and now in 1955 it might have been possible to repeat this. Remember that at this time there were threats of atom bombs raining down on cities, and perhaps this might have moved a few more people.

But families follow jobs growth, and the good jobs were in the city. So at the very time these calls were being made to restrict the size of the cities, these cities responded by starting to grow at faster and faster rates. Most major cities have grown at least threefold in a period of 60 years, far outstripping the population growth.

About 40 years ago, a number of experiments were tried to make places like Bathurst in NSW into regional growth centres. A number of Departments sent some of their workers to live there, and money was poured into infrastructure in the region. But as governments changed, so too did the political will. Now, the whole concept seems to be forgotten, for all practical purposes.

So, unless a Japanese submarine gets into the harbours of our seaboard cities and starts to shell the suburbs, or something equally preposterous happens, I suspect the drive to the city will just continue – even allowing for the oldies and grey nomads who sell up and move to the coast or their caravans for their retirement.

# OCTOBER NEWS ITEMS

A Political Science Professor at the Australian National University said today that "Australians live precariously on the sea-cooled fringes of a **vast, desiccated, bleached, eroded wilderness, a worn-down continent**"….

He was speaking at a national conference that discussed the **creation of a new State in northern Australia**. "We have more than our fair share of **politics and politicians** because of inter-governmental bickering and political irresponsibility. **A new State would spread, even more thinly than at present, the limited resource of statesmanlike talent.**"

All the States are considering **one-man buses**, but are being hampered by the **fears of the Unions that job losses will occur**. On October 4th, the NSW Government **decided to force a showdown** and will soon introduce the buses on 18 routes. **Expect fireworks.**

**The winner of the Redex Trial was finally announced. It went to a Volkswagen**, and was awarded after a series of appeals. **Two previous winners had been announced, but had lost out in the appeals**. Future trials will be restricted to only 15 days, and cover only the eastern States.

**Australian troops bound for Malaya** in *HMAS Georgie* will be allowed **a ration of two bottles of beer a day**. One can be drunk before lunch, and the other in the evening. The beer will be duty-free. Cigarettes will also be duty-free. Big poker schools are banned, but **housie-housie is permitted.**

**Drive-in movies** are getting closer. The NSW Government issued nine licences to open outdoor theatres, and they must be operating **within a year**.

In Ulladulla, **the new bowling club has been frustrated** by miscreants who over-sowed **newly-sown greens with paspalum seeds**. This will delay the opening of the greens by two months

News item, October 19th. **The Leader of the Opposition, Dr Evatt, stunned the nation** when he addressed the House of Representatives tonight. He said that **he had written to the Soviet Foreign Minister and, in effect, asked him if Russia had any spies working in Australia,** and what they were doing. Molotov relied that there were none….

**The House was stunned for several seconds, and then erupted with laughter.** How could anyone ask the Russian Foreign Minister if they had spies? Of course they did. What would you expect Molotov to have said? Is this the way to conduct diplomatic matters? **Questions such as these proliferated, all of them derisive….**

**Comments were scathing.** One Liberal Member said we were witnessing "the sad spectacle of a great mind decaying." A Labor Member talked about himself "walking the streets looking for jobs"….

A few days later, Prime Minister Menzies announced that **Federal elections would be held on December 10th**. Menzies could have waited much longer, but after **the Evatt fiasco,** it seemed that an early election was very much in his favour. He was no doubt also influenced by the **very public ongoing internal squabbles that were apparent in the Labor Party** all through the year.

I remind you that apart from the squabbles in the Labor Party, **strikes** were still all over the place, our troops were steadily **going to Malaya**, and **international disputes** were ongoing. **They were just part of the background.**

**Ear-markings on sheep were inadequate** for proving ownership, so that it was very difficult for police to prove that sheep had been stolen. Also **livestock bookkeeping by most graziers was poor or non-existent**, and that made recovery and prosecution almost impossible.

The Royal Australian Navy is also seeking 1,000 naval recruits to serve in our Navy – from Great Britain. A new scheme will allow recruits to bring their families to live in Australia, and citizenship will become available after a time of service, if they want it.

Western Australia will introduce **heavy fines for the misuse of spearguns**, in and out of the water. It will be the first Australian State to do so.

The Sydney Surf Life Saving Association has recommended to the State body that **march-past events for women be allowed at surf-club carnivals**.

American audiences, in a national poll, chose James Dean as the actor of the year for his role in *East of Eden*. Dean was killed in a motor accident recently, and was mourned deeply by many Australian teenage girls.

## GREYHOUND TRAINING

The battlers in Australia were always looking for ways to get out of poverty. Some of them dreamed wildly about winning the lottery. Many youths dreamed they could have a go at boxing, and win a world title. Lots of others dreamed of owning a racehorse and winning the Melbourne Cup.

But every day, in the suburbs and country towns, you could see other battlers walking their one big hope of a fortune, **their greyhound dog.** Up at the crack of dawn, these ambitious trainers would cover miles and miles at a brisk pace until they were as lean as the hounds themselves. They fed them the best food, housed them in proper kennels, groomed them every day, responded with alarm to any sign of a malady and, I have heard it said, would on cold nights sleep with them.

The greyhound industry was going quite well at the moment, making a good come-back after the wartime restrictions on race meetings that had badly affected the industry. The number of meetings was substantial, the prizes were not too bad, and the number of dogs in training was increasing sharply.

However, there were a few complaints that said that all was not perfect.

**Letters, A Tonge, President, RSPCA, Sydney.** In respect to the cases of premeditated cruelty to cats by greyhound trainers, there is only one cure, heavy gaol sentences.

Only a sadist without any feeling would pull out a cat's claws and allow it to be then torn to pieces by greyhounds.

Why magistrates impose paltry fines for such savagery is beyond decent citizens' comprehensions.

I have asked the Chief Secretary to amend the law to provide a minimum gaol sentence of five years.

**Letters, J King.** I would like to point out, in fairness to the majority of dog owners, that the use of cats is not to be condoned.

Most owners find that the track greyhound is a far better chaser of the mechanical lure when his training is **devoid of all kills**. A greyhound by instinct will chase anything that moves, and nine out of 10 dogs will chase as soon as they see the lure get under way, even if it is their first acquaintance with it.

However, dogs coming from properties from which they have had plenty of natural game are always harder to break in than those that have seen very little of live kills.

While it is possibly true that some ratbags associated with the sport take a delight in giving their dogs kills, this definitely is not so with the majority of owners.

**Comment.** My eldest brother was one of the greyhound battlers. He would have supported Mr King above. He, and his hound clique, were opposed to blooding because after a dog had been blooded, it would not chase flat-out because it could smell the hare was not the real thing. In any case he, along with most trainers, were animal lovers, and had no truck with cruelty to cats.

## DRESSING FOR THE THEATRE

This little gem started animated conversations.

**Letters, Constance Howard-Blott, Secretary, Civic Pride Society, Sydney.** With grand opera and high-class theatre in the Sydney air, the time seems opportune to put forward a plea for better dressing in our theatre audiences.

With the present appearances of famous international stars of stage and opera, would it not be a gracious gesture to these great overseas artists if Sydney theatre-goers appeared in evening dress instead of the drab day dress habitually worn nowadays? If it is the "right thing" to wear evening dress on first nights, why discard it for day dress on all other nights at the theatre?

**Comment.** Such a neat little piece of snobbery was sure to get some people off-side.

**Letter, R Morrow.** Is Constance a real person? I spent some time researching the writer's posh name, and the society that she supposedly represented, to see if she was a real person. It occurred to me that this Letter was simply a wind-up, calculated to whip the masses into a state of bother. As a result I can neither confirm nor deny that the person really exists.

**Comment.** Yes, she is a real person.

**Letters, B R Lugg.** If I were behind the footlights, my favourite audience would be composed of ordinary commonsense people, whose main objective is entertainment and mental nourishment.

An audience, intelligently responsive and appreciative more than makes up for that lack of social splendour, which in many cases means exactly nothing.

**Letters, M W H.** Considering the "dressiness" of the female section of evening picture-goers in Sydney I agree with Constance Howard-Blott that the theatre audiences present a very drab scene indeed.

How very uninspiring for the actors and actresses to look out upon a sea of topcoats and everyday hats, instead of colourful evening dresses and scintillating jewels.

Sydney's womenfolk have a world-wide reputation for being smart – even, some say, over-dressed – so wake up, you theatre-going ladies!

**Letters, E Saunders.** Surely the visiting international stars like to see full houses, whether the audiences are wearing formal dress or not.   Would it be better for our prestige for them to play before half-empty houses, with all the patrons wearing evening dress?

I think it will be a very sorry day for the Australian theatre when people won't go to an opera because they haven't any evening dress.

**Letters, Harold Begg.** When "live shows" predominated, theatres were built to cater for every class of patron.

There was the "dress circle," if dress was desired, "stalls" for informality, and "gallery" where mixed parties enjoyed a "bob's worth of hangover."

**Letters, Constance Howard Blott, Sydney.** Your correspondents appear to think that correct evening dress for the live theatre is synonymous with vanity and mental vacuity.

**Correct dressing for various occasions comes under the heading of good manners**, and when that attire is attractive without ostentation it signifies good taste.   In my opinion, **both are virtues to be encouraged**, not faults to be condemned.

It is regrettable that those who deplore "dressing up" for festive functions have such a poor opinion of the mentality of theatregoers of the past, who, right up to comparatively recent times, and without exception, wore evening dress to the theatre.

**Letters, Margery Clarke.** While agreeing with Howard-Blott that dressing suitably for an entertainment is a form of good manners, and one to which I personally would very much like to subscribe, I should like to put the matter in this light.

I am a woman in the lower-wage bracket, obliged to live on what I earn, which means that my dressing has to be suitable for the office and street.

I am sure a great many people similarly placed happen to like opera. Does Miss Blott really think we should stay at home rather than offend her aesthetic eye?

**Letters, H E Ellen.** Your correspondent, Constance Howard-Blott, fails to take account of the fact that there has been a revolution, particularly among men, against arbitrary restriction in relation to dress. The man of today prefers ease and comfort to a rigid adherence to outmoded convention.

There are thousands of people who are keenly interested in music and drama who find it difficult enough to pay the current high prices of admission to theatres without incurring the extra expense involved in the process of keeping up with the Joneses and the Howard-Blotts in the matter of expensive, uncomfortable and unnecessary clothing.

Mrs Howard-Blott is thinking in terms of an era that has departed, and risks having her name immortalised in the local field of culture as a parallel to that of Colonel Blimp in the military field.

## HITCH-HIKING IN AUSTRALIA

About 60 years ago, I was a student. When one set of term holidays came round, myself and two others set out to hitch-hike to Queensland and back. This was not at all unusual at the time, lots of students did it, and motorists were quite ready to enjoy the company of young adventurers on their long journeys.

When we set off, the world was a nice, simple place. We made 120 miles in the first afternoon, slept of the bank of a river, and were ready for our next lift by eight in the morning. But, the world had changed overnight, because after dark the previous night, a motorist had stopped and picked up three male hitch-hikers, had driven twenty miles with them, and then they had murdered him, and taken all his goods. It was in the morning papers as screaming headlines, and stayed on the front page for a week.

The public outrage was immense. Here we have a good Samaritan, stopping to help out some young men, and they had then returned the kindness by killing him. It was not just this particular act that enraged the population. It was the realisation that one of Australia's long-established customs had been destroyed in one cruel act.

It was like the despair and sense of loss of innocence that swept the nation when a few years later, the schoolboy, Grahame Thorn, on his way to school, was kidnapped, a ransom was demanded and paid, but the child was killed anyway. It was straight out of an American B-Grade gangster film. Things like that just didn't happen in Australia. **Could any parent ever let their children walk to school again?**

Now, the question was whether any driver would feel safe to pick up hitch-hikers ever again. It was a loss of an Australian tradition, a feeling that somehow we were better off than our American friends, that was the real loss, and the feeling that every one of us was a loser.

Needless to say, the rest of our trip to Brisbane and back was difficult, and took us three times as long as we intended.

In fact we ended up jumping rattlers to finish it off. None of that harmed us in any way, but I can remember at the end we decided that from that day, hitch-hiking in Australia was dead.

It turned out that we were mainly right. If it persisted, it did so on a much smaller scale than previously, and only really dedicated risk-takers for some reason offered or accepted lifts thereafter.

## HITCH-HIKING IN EUROPE

At the same time, a number of Letters appeared in the Papers concerning hitch-hiking in Europe. There were a few reports in a couple of newspapers that said that Australians on the road in Europe were no advertisement for Australia, and were often monosyllabic, ungrateful, and generally poor passengers.

**Letters, A W Jones.** Touring the British Isles and parts of the Continent by car, I often felt disgusted and ashamed to mention I belonged to Australia when I saw the droves of young people, many carrying Australian flags on their backs, thumbing for a free ride along the road.

This was heaviest on the Continent, though very prevalent in Scotland. We had the experience of taking two hitch-hikers for about 70 miles in France and when we drew into a town for the night their only feeling apparently was one of dismay that we were not going another 40 miles, where they would be able to get to a youth hostel.

It was apparently one's duty to pick them up. How we admired the boys and girls we met who had bought pushbikes and were doing it the hard but fun way.

**Letters, Cynthia Brahms.** As an Australian who has just returned after six years of residing in England, I was appalled to read Sir John Lienhop's statement.

The young Australians who hitch-hike do more good for Australia than any written propaganda – if any can be found in London! They usually are fine intellectual types who wish to see more of the world than did their parents' generation. One is, when young, always being lectured about the "adventurous spirit," which indeed these young folk possess.

Hundreds of motorists who have helped these young hitch-hikers on their way have been given an enthusiastic and true picture of life in Australia, of which otherwise they would never have known. I would say these youngsters are ambassadors and have succeeded in putting Australia favourably on the map not only in England but all over the Continent.

Go ahead, youth, and the very best of luck.

**Letters, (Miss) J Croker.** While the best way to get to know a country and its people is to live there for some time, this is not, for many young people, a practical consideration. The next best method is, quite definitely, to go hitch-hiking. One meets the transport-drivers, commercial travellers, doctors, in short, the people of the country.

In three months' hitch-hiking on the Continent last summer, we had lifts from people in all imaginable walks of life. Never once did we meet the attitude that what we were doing was harming Australia's prestige. Rather were we greeted with admiration for our pluck in determining to see their countries and to learn as much as possible about them.

**Comment.** It's hard to say, but probably they were no better or worse than humans generally.

# MURRAY CODS

**Letters, W A Grose, Burrinjuck Dam.** Could anyone tell me the size and weight of the biggest Murray cod ever caught here or within 60 miles up or down the river?

**Letters, J W Evans, Australian Museum, Sydney.** Mr Whitley, an expert, advises me that over a century ago Murray cod of up to 120lb in weight were caught in the Murrumbidgee.

It will further interest anglers to learn that very recently a special exhibit has been installed in the entrance hall of the Museum in which the greatest recorded lengths and weights of all large Australian and New Zealand fishes are listed.

According to this list, the Murray cod has been recorded up to 6ft in length and 182lb in weight.

**Letters, W G Noble.** A quarter of a century ago, with old mates, I camped on holidays during several years at Narrangullen on Burrinjuck Dam. We caught large numbers of cod, grunter bream, and yellow-belly perch.

The largest cod caught on all our trips only weighed 53lb, while several others weighed 25lb each. Only heavy rods and lines were used for cod with natural bait – speckled frogs, big white wood grubs, and yabbies (freshwater crayfish). No drum-nets, crosslines or other unsportsman-like devices were countenanced.

When I was a young **mounted police trooper** at Walgett in 1900, fishing a deep bend of the Namoi River, I landed a large cod five feet long. Weighed in the presence of the late Inspector Pountney and Sergeant Cameron, it turned the scales at 120lb.

Two years later, during the big 1902 drought, three bridge workmen camped at the four-mile crossing of the Barwon River, Walgett. Disturbed by a great commotion in the water at night, they discovered the cause to be an outsize cod chasing other fish.

They obtained a large hook made by a local blacksmith, baited it with lumps of kangaroo, then fastened it to fencing wire tied to a stake driven into the ooze. The monster was then lured to his doom.

Conveyed to town, it was weighed and proved to be just on 250lb.

It was exhibited in a marquee; the local **bellman** notified residents that 1/ would admit each one to view the giant, and the sum of 20 Pounds was raised for the local hospital.

**Comment.** One of the sad things in life is that the old bushman, with his many yarns, has just about disappeared. If ever you have been fortunate to have heard such a man talking, you will know that he always had a string of stories, that seemed to be wildly exaggerated at first, but as he talked more and more, and produced more evidence, he got increasingly convincing. In the end, listeners generally went away believing firmly in the unbelievable, and thrilled with themselves for having met and talked with such a widely experienced adventurer.

Now, I am not suggesting that the numbers in the above Letters are exaggerated. The Letter from the Museum would scarcely allow for that. And the Letter from Mr Noble has all the earmarks of accuracy. All that I am saying is that his way of spinning his story reminds me of the old master bushman story tellers, and that I am happy to sit at the feet of this widely experienced adventurer.

## NEWS AND VIEWS

**Letters, D H Walker.** I would like to make a plea, through your columns, for the introduction of daylight saving through the summer months.

Anyone who has lived in higher latitudes will know the pleasure to be had from being outdoors after tea at night and having an hour or so of light in which to garden, to stroll or to sit and enjoy the sunset.

Sydney's night falls quickly enough without having it as early as 6.30pm, as at present. It is light at 4.30am when most people have at least one more hour in bed to go. Why not put the clock back one hour and have that hour for daylight leisure?

**Letters, John T Dence.** The advocates of daylight saving obviously are unaware of the complications necessary to bring it into effect. For instance, they may not be aware that Sydney standard time is kept throughout Queensland, Victoria, and Tasmania. And as Cairns and Melbourne are nearly on the same longitude, there is a difference in the times of sunrise and sunset varying from 20 minutes in Cairns to over 40 minutes in Western Victoria.

On sun time, Melbourne is some 25 minutes behind Sydney, and before Federation travellers by train had to put back their watches on leaving Albury.

# NOVEMBER NEWS ITEMS

Princess Margaret issued a statement today that said she would not marry Group-Captain Peter Townsend. As third in line for succession to the throne, she was bound by the 200-year-old Royal Marriages Act that said she could not marry a divorced person. Only by renouncing her right could she have married him….

Leading Churchmen, Parliamentarians and most newspapers said today that she had averted a crisis involving the Church, Crown and State. The Times editorialised with "All the people of the Commonwealth will feel gratitude to Princess Margaret for taking the selfless Royal way which, in their hearts, they expected of her".

That horse race in Melbourne on the first Tuesday was won by Toparoa, the second favourite. The favourite was Rising Fast. The news reports of the race brought back old names: Neville Sellwood, Jack Purtell, and Tommy Smith. The prize-money for first was 10,000 Pounds.

In the first week of November, the Egyptian and Israeli armies fought fierce battles. The Suez crisis is getting closer.

The NSW Government has decided that an open, world-wide competition should be held to decide the design of the Opera House in Sydney. It will have two Australian judges, one from Britain, and one for Finland, all of whom were named.

News item, November 12th. The **Constituent Assembly of New England** (North East of NSW) will renew its **campaign for separate Statehood at a meeting here tomorrow.** Its main business will be a discussion of **the allocation of assets between the proposed new State and NSW.**

News item, November 19th. **The dispute over one-man buses is warming up.** From today, drivers who refuse to take the buses **will be dismissed**, rather than be suspended as in the last week. **A 24-hour strike** of all Sydney and Newcastle buses and trams **has been called for next Tuesday....**

Sure enough, the strike was held, but **much of its impact was lost because passengers were so accustomed to such actions.**

News item, November 28th. After **650 men had been dismissed** from three Sydney depots, **the Unions have agreed to cease industrial action** and accepted a deal that provided for **a trial period** for the one-man buses.

**Qantas has just completed a competition in the US** that asks entrants **to submit a name for a kangaroo** that it will use in its advertisements in the US. A Mr Wilson Siebert submitted "Sam" and for some reason, that name won. **The prize for the winner was a kangaroo....**

**The animal is about to arrive in America,** but the lucky winner lives in a city in a three-bedroom flat, and **does not know what to do with it.** Zoos will not accept it because they have enough roos already. So, at the moment, it is still a problem for him.

# STIPENDS FOR CLERGY

Perhaps an observer would be excused for thinking that, if the clergy were forsaking one of their traditional habits, the home visit, they might also be moving away from their many different vows of poverty, and be instead living the life of luxury.

**Letters, No Margin.** Today I received a treasurer's statement of receipts and expenditure for a Church of England in the western suburbs and was astounded to learn from it that the rector's stipend is 506 Pounds!

This rector is married with three children (there are probably others with heavier responsibilities) and how he can keep that little family fed and clothed on such a pittance is beyond imagination.

It is a lasting disgrace to a wealthy Church to have such mean regard for a servant with a cultured and expensive education. I venture to say that if it required the services of an uneducated youth of 16 it would not be able to secure one for 506 Pounds a year.

Astonishment turns to disgust when I think of necessities like oranges and apples at sixpence each, spinach at 4/6 a half bunch, eggs at 6d each, and milk 11d a pint for a family of five, to say nothing of meat, fish, clothing, schooling, dental attention, and a hundred and one other needs.

Surely, the Lord must provide.

**Letters, Anglican Cleric.** In bringing the question of stipends before the public, "No Margin" has done a great service to many clergy.

The facts as stated are certainly correct, except that the reference to "a wealthy Church" is not quite fair.

A study of any Church treasurer's statement will show that the rector's stipend is governed largely by the contributions of the people through the offertory plate and by other means.

The 2/ piece is still the main contribution made in church, and until church people realise that this equals about 6d of 20 years ago and then multiply their 2/ by at least four, the unfortunate rectors and their families will continue to be the sufferers.

The Church has often been called "wealthy" because it owns property, but mostly this property is used for church purposes, and is not income-producing. Property which is let yields very little after rates, insurance, and very heavy repair bills (most Church property is old), and other items are met.

In any case, all real property and other assets of the Church are held on trusts for special purposes, and these trusts cannot, of course, be breached in order to help underpaid clergy.

The clergyman is only as poor as the congregation of his church allows him to be.

**Letters, E T.**  Referring to the letter, "Rector's Stipend", your correspondent may not be aware that the cleric in receipt of 506 Pounds per year, does live rent free, also telephone, gas, electric light are paid by the parish council of the said church.

Weddings (and, I think, funerals these days) are all extra to his salary.  In some churches the weddings would be worth another 100 Pounds to 200 Pounds a year, and doctors as a rule do not make any charge to ministers of religion.

**Letters, Rector, Milson's Point.**  "No Margin" rightly calls some stipends low, but the Church of England in Sydney is certainly not "a wealthy Church," except perhaps in capital value of unproductive property.

While active Anglicans stand any comparison in generosity, the Church's actual income per head is probably lowest of any denomination, due to its greater overburden of nominal members who contribute nil.

It has no State aid (as many think), and no central fund to pay clergy. Individual parishes must not only pay their own way in full; they also pay some 15,000 Pounds p.a. to support the diocesan organisation.

Every rector, before he accepts a parish, is told its average income and his stipend, and must budget accordingly.

My own income has averaged 430 Pounds p.a. over the past nine years, simply because the parish could afford no more.

**Letters, Free Church Cleric.** I **would prefer** to purchase my own home, live in the suburb of my own choice, and pay my home off with an allowance equal to the value of the rent of the house I occupy.

One thing faces me that E T (and others who think like him) should consider. When I retire – and that is not such a great way off now – I must vacate the rent-free home and find a home of my own. To do this, **I must save the price of my home, 3,000 Pounds, from my basic wage stipend**. I would like E T's advice on how to do it.

My parish is a large and semi-industrial one. I have to provide my own transport, a car; and after receiving a travelling allowance to run it, I find myself from 50 Pounds to 75 Pounds per year out of pocket.

If I officiate at a funeral, I am aware that the driver of the mourning coach and the grave-digger are more highly paid than I am. A girl of 20 years of age in my congregation gets within a few shillings a week of my stipend. A young fellow after two years' training as a school-teacher starts on a salary in excess of mine.

E T's suggestion of 100 Pounds to 200 Pounds per year for weddings leaves me a bit envious. Over 20-

odd years of ministry I could not average 25 Pounds per year. As for funerals, one does not look for any remuneration, though some people insist on expressing their appreciation in a tangible way. In my ministry I have not averaged 5 Pounds per year in this way.

E T has rightly stated that doctors do not make a charge to ministers of religion. I assure him that the clergy are sincerely appreciative of this generous consideration by the medical profession.

**Letters, C F M.** In the most informative article on the stipends of clergy, it was stated that, "Like any other members of the Church, the rector is expected to contribute his tithe, one-tenth of his income, to Church work."

I venture to suggest that this is the root cause of the whole problem.

While it is a laudable and scriptural principle to give one-tenth of one's income to the work of God, it would seem that the Church, collectively speaking, is not observing this principle of giving, otherwise she would not be in the financial predicaments through which she is now passing.

It is well to remember that the two-shilling piece, so often given by parishioners as their weekly offering, is only one-tenth of one pound, and about one one-hundred-and-thirtieth of the average wage today. Therefore, the problem is one which only Church people themselves can solve by proper and direct giving to the work of God.

**Comment.** It seems that the clergy were not spending church funds on wanton displays of luxury. In fact, it seems that they were quite prepared to live off the old fashioned smell of an oily rag.

# THE C of E  AND DIVORCE

Princess Margaret had always been seen as a bit of a rebel compared to her sister Elizabeth. Not that she was some sort of tearaway, just a little bit wilful. While her sister filled the role of heir apparent to the throne, and always acted in a thoroughly responsible manner, Margaret seemed a little wilder. In her late teens, and early twenties, she reportedly attended parties where some of the other guests were not so well accepted by society, and where the behaviour was not what you might expect in the staid world we imagined that she lived in.

More recently, she had spent much time in the company of Group-Captain Peter Townsend, a divorcee, and it would be reasonable to say that a deep affection developed between the couple. Over the last month, newspaper speculation had been intense, saying that the couple would become engaged to marry, despite the Church of England and British upper crust society saying that this was not possible. A week ago, it was reported that Margaret and her grandmother had a long heart-to-heart. A few days ago, the Archbishop of Canterbury spent some considerable time with her, and also over the week she had spent time with Townsend.

The net result was that she issued her statement saying that she would forsake marriage to Townsend, basically to avoid splitting the Church and royalty over the rights and wrongs of her marriage to a divorced man.

Whatever your views on this latter argument, you have to admit that by now she was not at all wilful or irresponsible, and this was an act of great self-sacrifice.

**In the Letters that flowed in**, this sentiment was echoed often, and though the arguments on the whole matter veered all over the place, the appreciation of her act was universal. But, in the limited space available to me, I have left out some paragraphs that spoke highly of this.

As I just said, the Letters poured in, for over two weeks. Some of them were sensible, some of them were not. I will give you a sample of both, and leave you to separate the one from the other.

**Letters, (Mrs) Joanna Ladds.** The controversy about Princess Margaret and Peter Townsend may perhaps do some good if only in bringing into the open the C of E's archaic rules about divorce.

Statistics prove that there are thousands of men in Townsend's position – young men whose wives have left them for other men. What does the Church suggest they do?

If it is wrong for them to marry again, then are they to live in hotels or boarding houses, or with relatives for the rest of their lives?

If the leaders of the Church of England think that young men left without their wives are going to remain celibate for the rest of their lives in order to take communion, then they know less of their own sex than is good or wise.

**Letters, M C Cooke.** Congratulations to the winners of the Princess Margaret-Townsend Contest. The Church leaders and others who have raised their voices in hypocritical condemnation of such a union must feel very proud, that once again they have forced their medieval influence into the lives of two persons in love.

Princess Margaret, no doubt, will be handed over in due course to some chinless fop with a weak solution of blue blood as the only qualification necessary for a suitable match.

**Letters, Mother.** As every woman will understand what it cost Princess Margaret to come to her brave decision, so will every mother who is trying to bring up her family with a proper understanding of their duty to God and society bless and admire her as a good example.

**Letters, Evelyn Legg.** I wonder how much concern is being given to the two young sons of Townsend, who are quite old enough to be adversely affected by the publicity which is part and parcel of their father's life.

These two completely innocent children seem to me to be the real victims of the Princess Margaret and Townsend affair.

**Letters, Myopic.** So Princess Margaret has made her decision – and wisdom has triumphed!

Congratulations to those who helped: the Church leaders who can so aptly quote from or forget to quote from, the scriptures; the followers of a creed that distinguishes not between innocence and guilt; the "responsible" types who have sacrificed such a lot to duty themselves; those who think that "the people's" laws are not good enough for Royalty; the lucky, silent millions who are able to share their lives with the ones they love.

As for the little princess who loved a man for his own sterling qualities – none offered to make any sacrifice for her happiness.

**Letters, H W Rogers.** In view of the opinions on divorce now being expressed in our papers, it might be well to get back to the basic cause of the Church's objection to divorce.

It is not the rule of the Archbishop of Canterbury nor yet of the Church itself. It is the definite statement of Christ Himself.

It is true that a number of clergy have proved themselves traitors to the Holy Scriptures in this respect, but they are a minority in the Church of England. Strangely enough, they are the very people who pride themselves on their loyalty to the Bible.

In the present case, many wild statements have been made because a highly placed and lovable lady is involved. But is no thought given to reasons why married couples part in the first place?

I do not think any reasonable wife leaves her husband nor husband his wife without some contributing factor on the other side. The so-called innocent party is rarely entirely guiltless.

**Letters, D A Car.** How do you find the "innocent" party in a divorce? Just as it takes two to make a marriage, so it usually takes two to make a divorce. The really innocent party is almost non-existent.

Legal "innocence" is based normally on technicalities. I know of more than one case, in my own limited experience, in which the legally "innocent" party was the ultimate cause of the divorce.

**Letters, Woman Lawyer.** My admiration for Princess Margaret is outweighed by great sadness that she should have been offered up on the altar of sacrifice to outmoded traditions.

Now that she has given up the man of her choice she may never marry. Perhaps that will please those pious men who are out of touch with the lives of their people.

The Churches, along with many others, appear to have lost sight of the fact that the laws of our land in certain cases allow divorce and remarriage and that these laws represent the wishes of the majority of the people and that they are made by the people's representatives.

When I told my little girl about the princess, she cried. Let us weep, too, for a twentieth century Princess, so unlike the princesses in the fairy stories.

**Letters, N F Babbage.** The simple and sublime Christian dignity of Princess Margaret's announcement throws into even grater relief the disgraceful behaviour of the majority of the press – which have been at her heels like a pack of yelping wolves.

One can only hope that the Princess may be granted that peace and happiness which the morbid sensationalism of the Press has done so little to foster, and which she so richly deserves.

**Letters, E G.** As one who does not share the Church's official views on divorce, but nevertheless agrees that this marriage was impossible, I commend the "Herald's" penetrating, responsible and reasonable leader.

However, its criticisms seem severe. It must be assumed that the issues involved were laid before the Princess at the time of Group-Captain Townsend's "banishment" and probably many times since.   The decision was taken "in the cruel stare of world publicity," but it need not have been so.

**Comment.** There were other, longer, Letters, mainly from high-up church officials and from academics. These people gave us many quotes from the Old Testament, from the New Testament, from Saint Augustine, from Thomas Aquinas, and various still-living churchmen. They also looked at the laws before the Royal Marriage Act was passed, the legislative intent of the lawmakers, the precedents that have been established or not established since, and current interpretations of the Act.

None of these helped at all. They more of less cancelled each other out. They also seemed out of date, and irrelevant, in mid-20$^{th}$ Century. The question was would the Royal Marriage Act, of 200 years ago, last forever? It was not something that came from the Testaments, there was no pretence that it had divine inspiration. It had been created by men, as fallible and under the normal pressures of the times as men always are. The western world was now witnessing divorce growing at a rapid rate, watching as no-fault-divorce was about to go on many Statute Books. Should then the Marriage Act remain static for all time, given that almost all else was in a state of constant flux?

**Most people** thought that it should not.

**Comment.** Margaret, the Royals and the Government were doubtless very conscious of the fact that, about twenty years ago, the then King of England, Edward VIII, abdicated the throne so that he could marry a Mrs Simpson, **a divorced woman**. This created a huge scandal at the time, and rifts occurred at all levels of society. Nobody wanted a repeat of that.

There is no happy ending to this particular story. Margaret and Townsend went their own ways. Margaret later married Anthony Armstrong-Jones in 1960, and they were divorced in 1978. She never remarried. She died in 2002.

# DECEMBER NEWS ITEMS

The Federal election will be held on December 10th. Prime Minister Menzies was spending a lot of time on **the hustings,** addressing audiences in town halls, sports fields and the like. **He was always roundly heckled,** but his supporters kept the baying Labor interjectors at bay. Of course, no one heard much of what he had to say, nor did they care. **It was just a good night out....**

**Evatt, the leader of the Opposition**, was also doing the rounds of public meetings. **He was very vulnerable because of his recent Molotov correspondence,** and hecklers did not let him forget it. He also backed down on a promise to drop the means test on old-age pensions....

**This was the last time that Australia was to witness a round-the-nation old-style Federal campaign** where candidates **stumped** their way making promises to their electors at public meetings. **By the next election, TV was well established**, and voters were able to shout abuse at candidates from the comfort of their lounge. Crowds fell off election after election, and have now stopped coming, except for a few show-piece performances.

News item, December 2nd. A man walked quietly into the third floor of a doctors' practice in Wickham Terrace in Brisbane where the doctor was talking to a patient. He put his hand into a small satchel that he was carrying, **pulled out a gun, and shot the doctor three times and killed him**. Two other doctors ran in, and **one of them was shot and killed, and the other wounded.**

The man then **detonated one of several sticks of dynamite he had planted, and thus killed himself**. A male patient attempted to douse one stick of dynamite, and **had two fingers blown off**. Police **referred to the man simply as a maniac**.

**Can you believe it? Rents in most Australian states had been frozen at 1940 levels for fifteen years**, initially as a war-time measure. **This was a great deal for renters but a terrible one for landlords**. Rents had stayed fixed at this level because there were **more renters that landlords**, and politicians wanted to keep the majority happy....

Now, **Victoria has altered the Landlord and Tenants Act so that rent increases of up to 25 per cent will be allowed**. Other States did not immediately follow suit, and in fact **it took NSW a full decade before it made any major changes**.

**The election results are in**. The Liberal Party won in a landslide, with **Menzies picking up a cool 20 new seats in the House**. Evatt showed he was losing his grasp by saying that **Menzies had won "temporarily"**.

**"Sweltering Christmas Crowds Set Shopping Day Records"**. Shoppers were prosperous, more than 100,000 crowded the city stores. A few fainted or were trampled, hundreds were jammed and could not move, children were lost, women fought over a few scarce items, trams and buses were impossible, and trains were delayed going home by lightning and storms. **Christmas is such a wonderful time of the year.**

# TOP OF THE POPS, 1955

| | |
|---|---|
| Rock Around The Clock | Bill Haley |
| Only You | The Platters |
| Cool Water | Frankie Lane |
| The Great Pretender | The Platters |
| If I Give My Heart To You | Doris Day |
| That Old Feeling | Frankie Lane |
| The Yellow Rose Of Texas | Mitch Miller |
| Let Me Go, Lover | Joan Weber |
| Ballad Of Davy Crockett | Bill Hayes |
| Memories Are Made Of This | Dean Martin |
| Learnin' The Blues | Frank Sinatra |
| 16 Tons, What Do You Get? | Tennesse Ford |
| Love is a Splendored Thing | Four Aces |
| Autumn Leaves | Roger Williams |

## BEST RATED US MOVIES, 1955

| | |
|---|---|
| Daddy Longlegs | Fred Astaire, Leslie Caron |
| Blackboard Jungle | Glen Ford, Sydney Poitier |
| The Desperate Hours | Humphrey Bogart, Frederick Marsh |
| Man With The Golden Arm | Frank Sinatra, Kim Novak |
| Picnic | William Holden, Kim Novak |
| I'll Cry Tomorrow | Susan Hayworth, Richard Conte |
| It's Always Fair Weather | Gene Kelly, Cyd Charisse |
| Francis In The Navy | Donald O'Connor, Martha Hyer |
| East Of Eden | James Dean, Julie Harris |
| Marty | Ernest Borgnine |
| A Man called Peter | Richard Todd |
| Lady and the Tramp | Walt Disney |
| To Hell and Back | Audi Murphy |

# GOD AND JULIAN HUXLEY

Since before the start of the 20th Century, western society had been arguing whether the world and mankind had been created by a (Christian) God, or whether it had **evolved** over millions of years into what it is today. This argument had waxed hot and cold for decades and needless to say, nothing definite had been decided. I think it is true to say that more people in 1955 doubted the existence of an all-powerful God who was pulling the stings, and probably the numbers of doubters increased over time as scientific education gradually permeated more of society after the war.

But that is not to say that the Creationists were out of the argument. Nor that the argument was over. I give you a brief series of Letters that followed from statements by Britisher Julian Huxley, grandson of the famous Aldous Huxley, that were pushing the **evolutionary** line.

**Letters, H E Morgan.** Professor Huxley says, "it will be as impossible for a man who claims to be educated to believe in God, as it is now for him to believe in a flat earth."

It is time we had a card ready to hang around the necks of Professor Huxley and his kind. This card should bear the legend, "I am a living example of the stupidity of the text-book scientist."

There are two ways of accounting for the Universe, just as there are two ways of accounting for the Sydney Harbour Bridge, that it was built according to plan or that the whole thing shaped itself and threw itself across the Harbour.

**Letters, J A McCluskie.** Professor Julian Huxley does not know what is on the other side of the moon, but he does know where God is not. Clever Professor Huxley!

**Letters, Irene Allen.** Professor Julian Huxley deserves the thanks of all "thinking men." It is surprising to hear the anger he has aroused in numerous ordinary people who, as a rule, do not make public their belief in God.

We are too prone to take things for granted and show a lackadaisical attitude to our beliefs. So let us be thankful to him for making us get up and fight!

**Letters, R F C.** H E Morgan and J A McCluskie have taken Professor Huxley's statement in the wrong way.

As a scientist, he argues first and foremost from a standpoint of logic. From this premise he finds belief in God impossible; nevertheless, it is a fact that many people have felt the need for a power higher than themselves to whom they can turn.

I am sure Professor Huxley would not suggest that these people should give up this faith. But he points out that it will become logically irreconcilable with scientific thought and education.

If, by his forthright statements, he can prevent the next generation from growing up into such a rut as the present, if he can help a few young people to question beliefs, scientific, religious or otherwise, instead of blindly accepting them, then I for one say "Thank you, Professor Huxley."

**Comment.** I will not weigh in on the evolution versus creation debate. **In fact, I am happy to say that, even if I was so foolhardy, no one would take any notice of me.**

I will say, though, that it was noticeable that there was no scope for compromise between the writers, and no way that they would **hear** each other. They appear to be all set in their ideas, and nothing will change them. I expect that if the writers were still alive 60 years later, they would stick to their 1955 opinion. Such, it seems, is often the nature of religious debate, or slanging.

## TV IS COMING

TV will be introduced to Australia next year, in time for the Olympics. Very few people here had any experience at all with this wonderful new device, and so questions about how it would come to market abounded. I give you a sample of what was being asked, and the comforting reply.

**Letters, J P Kelly.** When television receivers become generally available to the public, will it be possible to purchase a set without having to pay additional money for unwanted features such as built-in radiogram and elaborate cabinet?

**Letters, W G Simpson, EMI (Australia) Pty. Ltd., Sydney.** Experience has proved that is more economical to own a separate receiver for radio and a separate receiver for television. Radio and television are distinct and different services. Due to the very short wavelengths on which television operates, a radio receiver cannot be used for television, and a television receiver cannot be used for the reception of radio programmes.

When television receivers are offered for sale in Australia, buyers will have the choice of table models, consolettes, consoles and de luxe models incorporating radio and gramophone, to meet their own individual requirements.

## WASTING TIME ON THE JOB

The *SMH*, stirred by reports of government workers loafing on the job, put an undercover reporter into Sydney's Eveleigh railway yards as a Laborer. His task was to observe just how much time the workforce spent in doing their job, and how much was spent idling.

His report was damning, and said that about one quarter of their time was wasted, and that the quality of their work was quite unsatisfactory. The sample of the ensuing writings below will give you an idea of how serious the problem was.

**Letters, E J Vickery.** I was apprenticed to fitting and machining at the Carriage Works, Eveleigh, until I resigned in 1953, after four months' service. During that time I saw how little work was being done for the Railways and how much was being done for the men themselves. The amount of work allocated to each tradesman and apprentice for each day could have been completed by morning tea. For the rest of the day the employees were able to do what they wished.

The younger apprentices are encouraged to "go slow" and are drawn into long conversations with the older employees. This is not stopped by the sub-foremen, who, in most cases, couldn't seem to care less.

Of the many Railway employees I have worked with, I have only known a couple who have been keen workers, but they are being continually heckled by the rest of the staff. I think many of the employees work harder trying to avoid work than they would need to if they did a day's work. I have also witnessed many dangerous practical jokes, and have seen tools being stolen from the workshops.

**Letters, Conscientious Worker.** My employment has recently taken me to an estate under the care of NSW Government. This estate is at present being re-painted by Public Works Department painters. Out of a working day of eight hours 30 minutes, these men waste four hours 40 minutes (both stated periods allow an hour for lunch). The working day is made up as follows:-

Arrive at job, 7.30am; commence work, 7.40; morning tea, 8.40-9.20; smoko (rest period), 10-10.30; cease work (preparation for lunch), 11.30; lunch, 11.45-12.45; resume work, 1pm; smoko (rest period), 1.20-2; cease work (preparation for quitting job), 2.50; leave for home, 4pm.

Each of these painters works only 19 hours 10 minutes a week.

**Letters, Diesel.** As one who recently completed a tour of inspection of the workshops I can assure the Minister, the Commissioner and Dr Ross that the report is unfortunately authentic.

The flagrant waste of time and apparent lack of supervision observed during the tour were disgusting. The apprentice guide remarked, however, that the men usually refrained from horseplay and looked busy when white collar strangers were seen as these visitors could be "brass hats."

**Letters, Ajax.** Some time ago I was called as an expert at an inquiry at Chullora Workshops. Operatives were taking 24 man-hours to do a task which departmental officers contended could be comfortably accomplished in 22 hours. The union challenged this assessment.

After making myself thoroughly conversant with all relevant conditions and conducting searching tests, I stated positively and unequivocally that 16 hours was a generous time allowance for the work in question. This contention caused such a storm of protest from union officials that, although I am over 70 years of age, I offered to personally prove that I could do the job in the time. I was not taken up on that issue.

Further, the quality of the work which I inspected in the railway shops would not, under any circumstances, be accepted by private industrialists as conforming to a reasonable standard.

**Comment.** Government, and in fact, all industry, had their hands tied. If an employee was really slacking, and management wanted to sack him, they needed to produce a smoking gun. That is, only if the offence was so blatant, that the Union could not publicly defend their member, would the sack be imposed. Otherwise, the Union would call a strike, and demand re-instatement. Offenders knew this, and were cunning enough to adjust their behaviour so that they never were really caught red-handed.

## SUMMING UP 1955

The main **international concern** for Australia was the situation in Malaya and thereabouts. As Menzies and the Americans saw it, the Red Menace had to be stopped there, before it swept through the region. Many Australians thought any threat was too far away, and did not see the need to fight them there. Still, we continued to send troops and arms to the region, and given that the Army could not recruit enough men, we would soon send conscripted National Servicemen as well. Some of these, reluctant soldiers in the first place, would become reluctant overseas fighters, and then be killed, at the age of 20. All for an involvement that was not popular at home.

The second international situation that would worry us was in the Middle East. I scarcely mentioned the Israeli-Egyptian growing conflict, but events would spiral, and 1956 would see a Suez Crisis that would give all the major powers a chance to flex their muscles. Our own Mr Menzies took the opportunity to strut on the world stage, but sadly for him, he ended up waddling instead.

**Within the nation, strikes were most obvious**. I spared you most of the every-day detail, but the most apparent fact was that there was no serious attempt to stop them. The Government did have the Crimes Act and other legislative powers to crush the Labor and Trade Union movement, but it mainly did not.

**It may have been** that Menzies and Co had a genuine regard for the right to strike, and took the liberal approach that industrial conflict is part of the realities of industrial life. **Or it may have been** that every strike provided an opportunity to belt it up the Communists and their so-called friends in the Labor Party. **It was probably an ever-changing opportunistic mix of these two**, but in any case, the strike situation was as bad at the end of the year as at the start.

As for the ordinary family of a mum and dad and three small children, things were pretty good. Any able-bodied man who wanted a job could get one, and he could crawl to his bank manager until he got a housing loan. Most people could buy a car on hire-purchase, and they were now saving for a deposit on a TV set. There was plenty of affordable sport for the whole family, plenty of beer for those who wanted it, and lots of Sunday barbies. If occasional thoughts of overseas disasters filtered through, then we would handle those **if they really did come close**. So, times were good, and the future promised to be as good or better.

But there was something about the world that we were leaving behind that appealed to me. The Letter below sums it up, I think.

**Letters, Miss Elizabeth Randall.** For some years I have each morning fed a carrot to the baker's carthorse near my office. His ears would shoot up, and his very tail quiver. He would give me, in his way, his views on life and philosophy, and I, in my way, would give him mine, as I whispered in his ear.

He has now gone, and his place is taken by a motor truck, which has no views on life and philosophy and to which it is impossible to feed a carrot.

This is doubtless progress. But as I look about the world now, I wonder if humanity would not be the better for less technical efficiency, and more warm, human feelings – less petrol and more oats.

Miss Randall has hit the nail on the head. She could see that the world in future would be different and probably better for the inevitable changes. Still, some of the old world was good too, and it was with reluctance that she let it go. That's how it was with me. You will have seen **that** throughout this book when I sometimes let nostalgia run rampant. I hope that you too have remembered your own bits of history, and that you get a chance to talk to your loved ones about them.

In 1958, the Christian brothers bought a pub and raffled it; some clergy thought that Christ would not be pleased. Circuses were losing animals at a great rate. Officials were in hot water because the Queen Mother wasn't given a sun shade; it didn't worry the lined-up school children, they just fainted as normal. School milk was hot news, bread home deliveries were under fire.

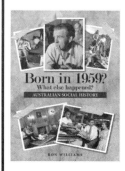

In 1959, Billy Graham called us to God. Perverts are becoming gay. The Kingsgrove Slasher was getting blanket press coverage. Tea, not coffee, was still the housewife's friend. Clergy were betting against the opening of TABs.

******************

Chrissi and birthday books for Mum and Dad and Aunt and Uncle and cousins and family and friends and work and everyone else.

Don't forget a good read and chuckle for yourself.

Born in 1939?
What else happened?

Australian Social History

Ron Williams

IN 1939. Hitler was the man to watch. He bullied Europe, he took over a few countries, and bamboozled the Brits. By the end of the year, most of Europe ganged up on him, and a phony war had millions of men idling in trenches eating their Christmas turkeys. Back home in Oz, the drunkometer was breathless awaited, pigeon pies were on the nose, our military canteens were sometimes wet and sometimes dry. Nasho for young men was back, Sinatra led his bobby-soxers, while girls of all ages swooned for crooner Bing.

********************

AVAILABLE AT ALL GOOD STORES

AND NEWSAGENTS